HOW TO ELECTRO ETCH

TUMBLERS, TOOLS, AND KNIVES

Easy To Make Etching Machines
and Stencils For Decorating Steel

Don Rathbun

Useless Bits Press

Contents

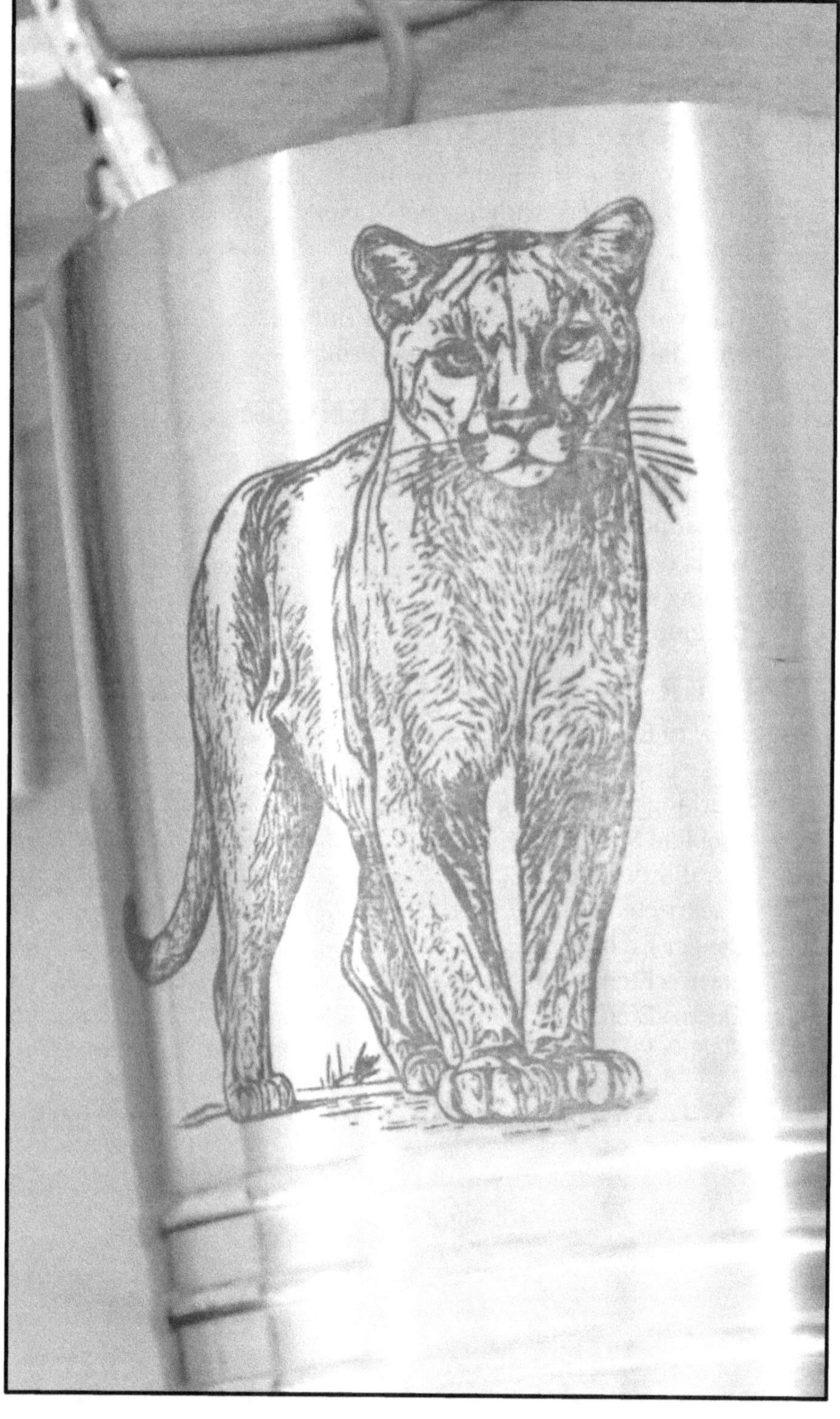

Introduction

This book is all about taking perfectly good stainless steel tumblers, tools, and knives, and making them better, or not.

Electro etching is a mostly one way street, and once your art has been applied to the steel, it takes a lot of work and sometimes skill to remove it. That said, it's also a very creative way to decorate bare stainless steel with all kinds of artwork.

Electro etching uses low voltage electricity but don't let that fool you. Use a resistor like the book says so you don't melt wires, burn fingers, cook stencils, and make your electronics smoke.

You can make a machine with power adapters, tool batteries, regular batteries, transformers, and more. The main machine is 12V 2A and will etch and mark; I show you how to make other machines, like a 3V machine from AA batteries that will etch, and also some more adventurous machines. The main machine involves stripping some wires and using a screwdriver; a $10 wire stripper is the only tool you might need to buy or borrow to make it.

Stencils were the hard part of electro etching, and this book makes them easy with thermal stencils, along with how to make more traditional screen stencils and a little on vinyl stencils.

See my website www.ElectroEtchDIY.com exploring electro etching, how-to guides, and photos; plus the latest links and searches to use for buying the parts and supplies in this book.

Let me know if you find any errors so they can be fixed, or a topic that really needs to be explained better, or maybe added, and if you find this book useful, post a review online to help get the word out.

I hope you enjoy electro etching as much as I have.

Don Rathbun
don@etchdiy.com
www.electroetchdiy.com
Useless Bits Press
May 2024

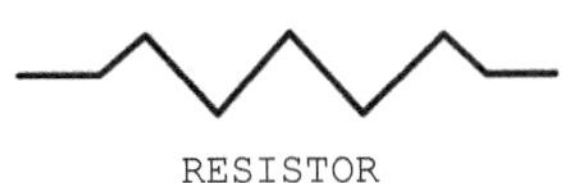

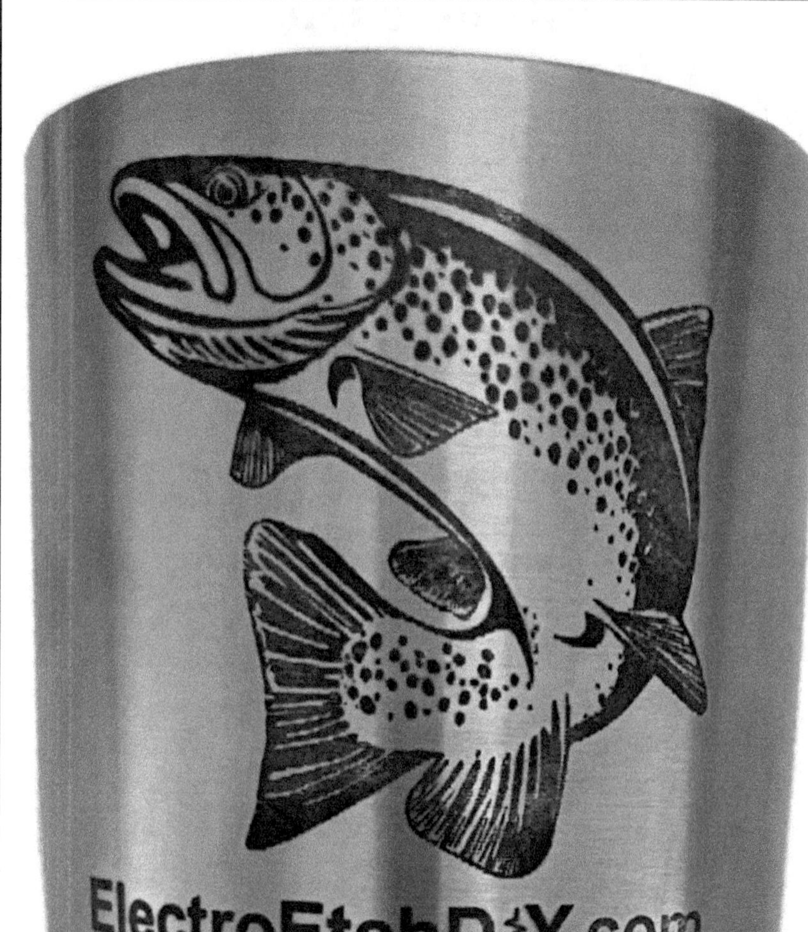

ElectroEtchDIY.com

Chapter 1 - Electro Etch DIY

Electro Chemical Etching

Have you ever wanted to decorate a steel tumbler for yourself or as a gift? How about putting your name or initials on a knife, or on tools, or make name tags for a keychain or the dog collar? Electro etching is an easy and inexpensive way of putting artwork and text on all kinds of stainless steel, and this book will show you how to assemble an electro etch machine using a 12V adapter, and make stencils for etching and marking steel. No electronics skills or soldering needed.

Voltage Required
You can etch with just 3V DC and mark with just 6V AC. We will build a machine that will etch and mark with 12V, and a machine that will etch using two AA batteries. You can also use a transformer, a spare or thrift shop adapter, or retrofit your existing machine.

Describing a Mark vs Etch
The electro chemical etching we are doing has two flavors, a mark and an etch. A mark adds a dark color, and an etch cuts. There are other names people call them that mean the same thing, but I like mark and etch because they describe the results; a dark mark, or, an etch into the metal. The patterns can be simple, or very detailed. Both are called electro etching or electro chemical etching.

What Does a Mark Do?
A mark will darken the surface, and barely etches a shadow into the steel. The color ranges from deep black to gray to brown, depending on the steel, electrolyte, voltage, and watts. A mark works with AC, and it's pretty fast. It will never chip or scrub off, but can be polished and sanded off. The facing page photo of a tumbler is decorated with a mark, the art is off Etsy, and a thermal stencil was used.

What Does an Etch Do?
An etch will cut into the surface. It ranges from barely there, to pretty deep. An etch on steel only works with DC, and the longer the dwell time, the deeper the etch. It will never chip or scrub off, but it can be sanded out eventually. The etches and marks of today will be on your steel tumblers, tools, and knives in a 100 years.

Buying Parts & Resources

See my website www.electroetchdiy.com for the latest recommended parts and supplies, and where to buy them.

Making an Electro Etch Machine

The chapter on electro etch machines will show you everything you need to make a DIY electro etch machine; no drilling, sawing, schematics, or soldering required. Learn to take insulation off the end of some wires, turn some screws, and you can make an etching machine. The recommended machine uses an adapter that is easy to get and very safe, and no, we will not crack it open.

Cost of a Machine

The cost of making the recommended machine is pretty reasonable. Buying online from Jameco.com in 2024: the adapter ($14), wire stripper ($8), diode thingy ($0.59), plus reasonable shipping. The terminal block ($15 for four on Amazon), a small halogen bulb (2 for $7), or roll of Nichrome wire ($7), and fuse ($5 for several), wire ($6 a roll), and a box o' clips and clamps ($12). Most etching and marking works really well with saltwater and some vinegar or sometimes baking soda, and you can use any water, any salt, and regular 5% white vinegar. You can salvage a handpiece graphite rod from a carbon zinc D battery ($1), or get larger graphite blocks online ($15); the craft aisle felt is great for the pads ($0.49). The whole thing will fit in a shoe box, and maybe costs less than the shoes did. If you are more confident with assembling things and electricity, there are chapters on how to use adapters, transformers, batteries, or a bench power supply, and how to retrofit your existing machine if it does not control power. That last bit "control power" is the key to using all sorts of power sources up to 30V, even massive car batteries.

Making Stencils

The chapters on stencils are all about making them yourself. The stencil has always been a hard part of electro etching. It is a pattern that controls where your artwork will mark/etch. It lets electricity and electrolyte pass, or blocks it. Before you invest in stencils, make sure your etching machine controls it's power, otherwise, you will not have consistent results (read the next chapter, even if you have a machine). This book shows you how to make stencils that are easy, fast, and consistent. You can make stencils to put your name on a knife blade, or large ones to decorate a gallon jug, and you can do one-off work for friends, family, and funds.

I will explain making impact stencils, making vinyl stencils, making screen stencils (the most well known), making thermal stencils (my favorite), and what makes each one useful. Even making thermal stencils from art on white paper. The kind of stencils you choose will depend on what your art looks like, the kinds of etching projects you are doing, and how much etching you plan to do. You can order custom stencils from several places if you just need a few.

If you get set up with thermal stencils and a thermal printer you can make many hundreds of stencils before buying more supplies. For making screen stencils, you'll buy screen film and a UV LED panel, and buy or make developer solution, then expose it and wash it out.

How to Electro Etch
The chapter on electro etching will explain how to etch and mark steel and fix common problems. The first part steps you through an etch and a mark. Once you've done that, you know you have a working machine and can move on to using stencils. With a good machine and stencils, electro etching is pretty easy. It will take practice to get the art right, line things up so they are straight, and get familiar with how long it takes to mark and etch with different size handpieces, pads, stencils, and steel.

History of Electro Etching
Electro etching has been around a long time. In 1840, some guys in the UK got a patent called "Engraving Metals by Voltaic Electricity". They coated a metal plate in varnish or a resist, scribed the design into it, dunked it in a tank, then added the voltaic part (electricity). It etched the metal plate so they could make prints; artists still use this technique, and they call the print an etching. Scribing a design into resist is slow, takes a lot of skill, and good resists are tricky. For a manufactured product, it wasn't until good stencils were available that many manufacturing companies could start to use electro etching on their production lines. Stencils like we use today were invented by companies from the electro etch industry, office printing, screen printing, sign making, and home crafts.

My Introduction To Electro Etching
I got hooked on electro etching a decade ago. My first try was with a little 9V battery, vinyl tape, saltwater, and a cotton swab, just like the videos. Cut shapes from the tape. Lay it down on the steel. Hook up the swab to an alligator clip, wet it with saltwater, and hook up the battery. Positive connected to the metal. Negative to the swab. Dab the swab across the stencil, and watch the bubbles and gunk build up. When I peeled the tape off and saw the etch cut into the surface, I was all in, and kept fooling with it. Fast forward through a crazy number of experiments, making electro etch machines from the schematics shared by knife makers (Thanks guys!), buying custom stencils and stencil materials (sometimes the wrong kinds), reading everything I

could find, ordering stuff to try out, making lots of mistakes, etching tumblers and knives and tools, production work, to today, and this book. The electro etch machine design in this book came from hundreds of builds and experiments until I got one that is simple to assemble (no soldering, no case, no drill, no switches), inexpensive, and reliable.

I didn't know I was going to write a book, but it sorta came together. My hope is it will make electro etching less expensive, more successful, and introduce it to a wider crowd.

What Will Electro Etch
Most kinds of steel will etch and mark, from the cheapest kitchen knife to the fancy stuff. The surface should be reasonably smooth, reasonably clean, and not have any coatings. If it is painted, powder coated, anodized, oxidized, galvanized, lacquered, rusty, dusty, or greasy, it probably won't electro etch properly.

Most other metals will etch and or mark using special electrolytes and sometimes different voltages. It's not always obvious what combination of voltage, electrolyte, and amps to use on a steel, and it takes experimenting; there are lots of kinds of steel. The main thing is to control the watts with a resistor so your stencil and machine stay healthy, and use a clean pad, and clean handpiece.

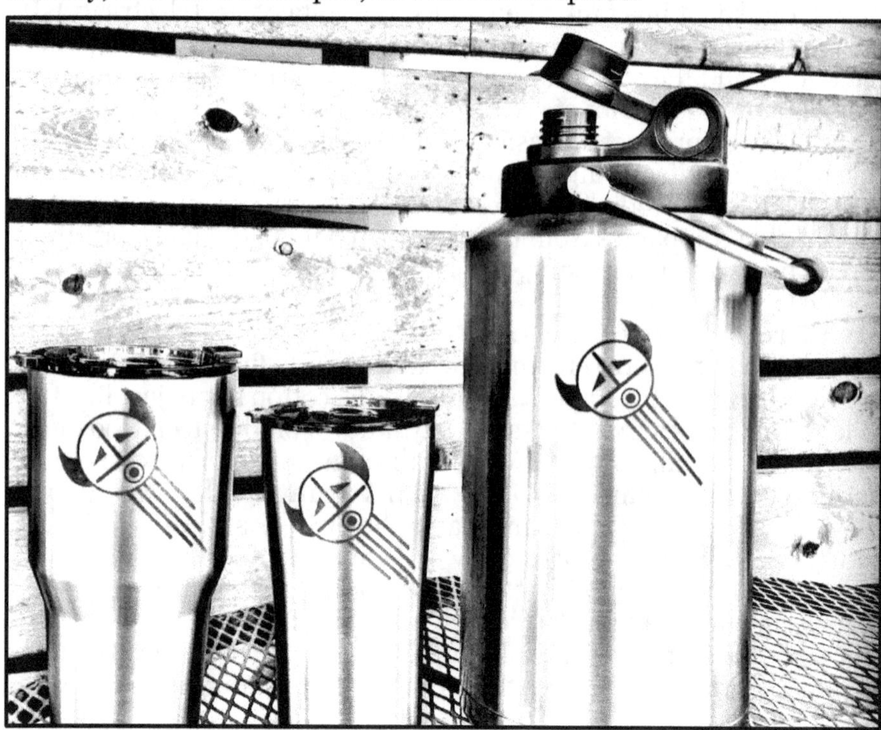

Electro Etching Safety

Safety - House Voltage & Low Voltage
Electricity from an outlet can hurt you, so make sure any connections between your electro etch machine and the outlet are well insulated and dry. Electricity from the etching machine is low voltage (officially 30V or less), but that does not mean you can ignore safety.

Safety - Power Source
Use the suggested adapter, or see the chapters on how to select an adapter, a transformer, or a battery.

Safety - Resistor
Always use a light bulb or wire resistor with your etching machine. The instructions make it easy to select a bulb or make a resistor.

Safety - Fuse
Always use a fuse with your etching machine.

Safety - Air Quality
Electro etching creates some fumes. Work in an area with ventilation. It smells like a hotel swimming pool since it's chlorine. A small fan can be helpful sometimes.

Safety - Water Pollution
Electro etching creates metal oxides. Wipe them up before you rinse, so they don't go down the drain, and don't rinse the pads in the sink.

Safety - Stains
The oxides will stain counters and clothing.

Safety - Gloves
It makes sense to use vinyl, latex, or nitrile gloves while etching. Officially, less than 30V will not hurt you, but there are exceptions like wet hands or scrapes and cuts that might cause problems.

Safety - Kids
Watch over kids and electro etching. Both for the safety around electricity and the creative things etching can do to your stainless.

Getting Started - The Shortest Path
Build an electro etch machine with the recommended parts, then get set up for making thermal stencils or if you have a Cricut or Silhouette cutter make some vinyl stencils. A thermal stencil was used for the mark on the jug and tumblers on the previous page.

The Basic Idea of an Etching Machine
A power adapter that makes 12V AC is connected to a terminal block that has a fuse, a resistor, and a diode. The resistor keeps the power under control and solves a lot of problems. The terminal block has two lugs that will hold an alligator clip. One lug is on the other side of a diode that makes DC so it will etch, and other lug is AC so it will mark. The handpiece is graphite with some felt, wet with saltwater and vinegar, and the stencil shown below is a thermal stencil. This version of the machine requires removing insulation from wire less than ten times and no soldering. Other versions can use battery power, an orphan adaptor, a transformer, or retrofit your existing machine so it works better by adding a resistor. Usually, I work over a plastic bag or a plastic tray so it's less messy, and have a paper towel to blot the handpiece so it's not drippy.

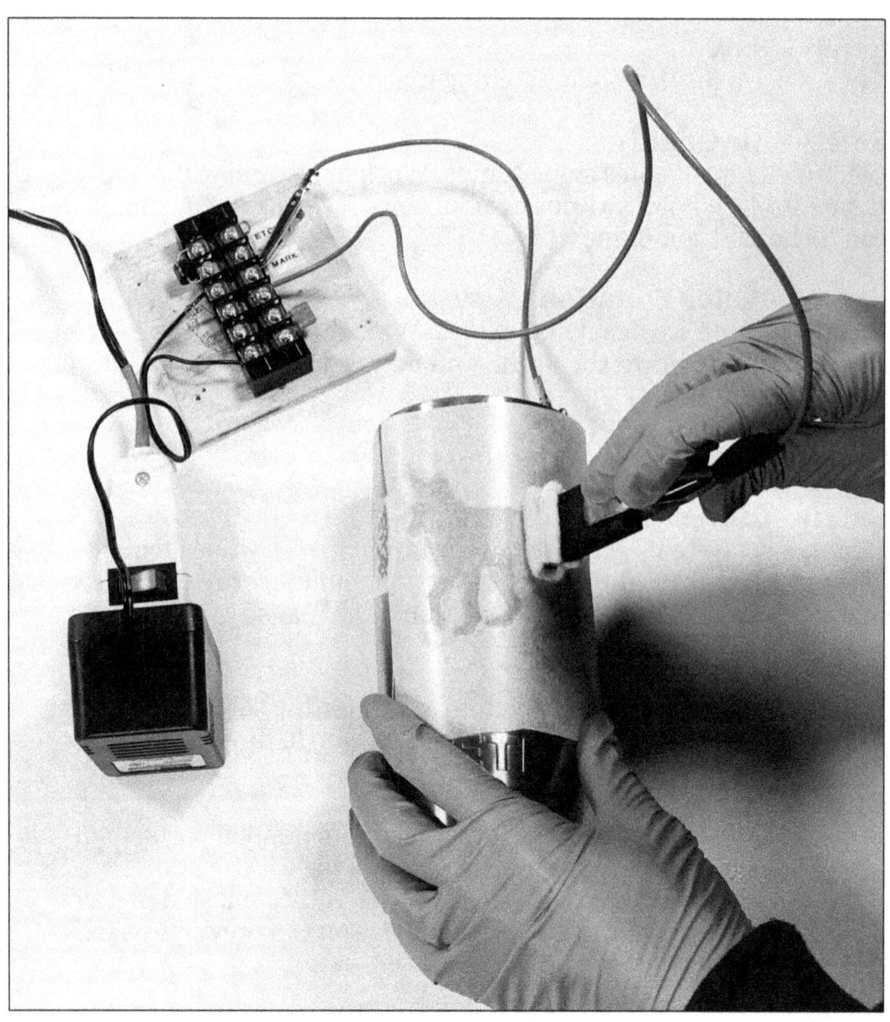

Etching

The etch below is a great little kitchen knife by Victorinox, made of high quality stainless steel. The letters are 1/10" high, and 2" long.

The text is not very large, but this size etch is easy with a thermal stencil or a screen stencil. Doing this with vinyl stencils is tricky to weed and keep the tiny bits inside the letters in place. Salt, vinegar and water was the electrolyte solution; it works for most steel. For deeper etching, a salt with baking soda electrolyte is good, and sometimes a store bought electrolyte is needed for some steels.

The resolution of the etch will only be as good as the art. The default resolution for many graphics programs is 72 DPI. If you change it to 300 DPI, your stencil will be crisper, and etches will be a lot nicer.

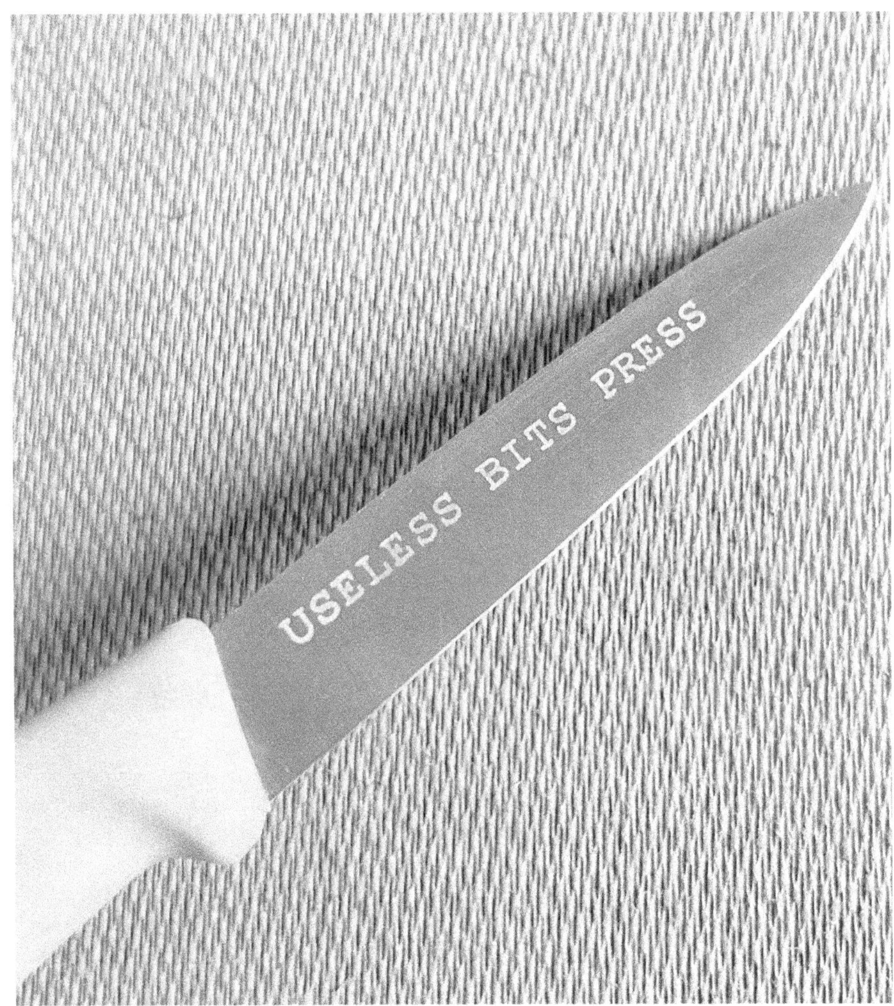

Battery Electro Etching

With a resistor, any battery between 3V and 30V will etch steel.
Without a resistor, you risk melting wires and even burning up a
battery, not to mention cooking your stencils.

The example below is using a couple of alkaline AA batteries, a wire
resistor, a fuse, and a handpiece made from the core of a carbon zinc
D battery. The base plate is stainless steel.

The stencil is a screen stencil that used oil soaked paper as a mask
and an inexpensive UV light. The tag is a test mark done with AC to
make sure all the parts of the art will show up. The machine design in
the next chapter will do etches and marks.

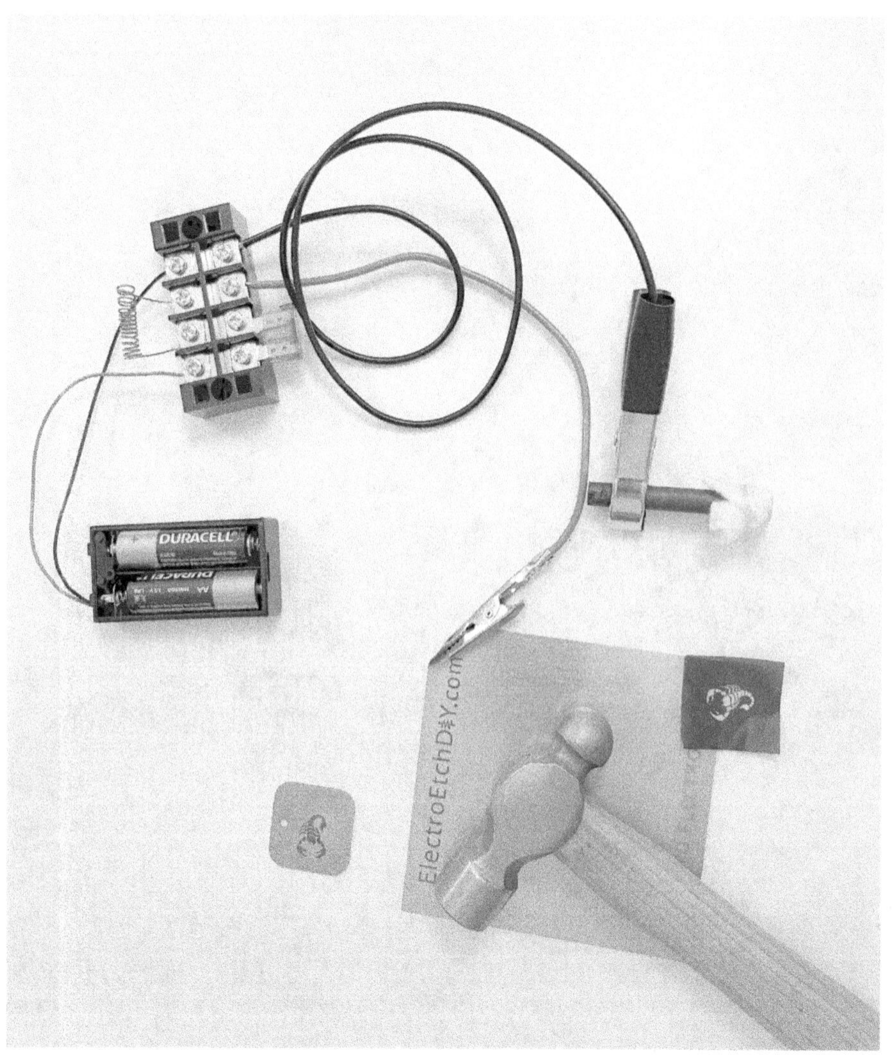

Etching a Tool

The ball peen hammer below was etched with the setup on the previous page, using 3V from two AA alkaline batteries. Using 3V is slow, and this etch was seven minutes.

To prepare this new hammer for etching, the protective coating had to be removed with solvent and elbow grease. A light coating of oil protects it from rust, and eventually it will turn dark like old tools do, but the scorpion etch will be there forever.

Most any tool with a small flat surface can be etched, but if it's plated, do a mark instead, since the etch will cut through chrome or nickel plating. The lower photo shows Pi and tiny tiny print.

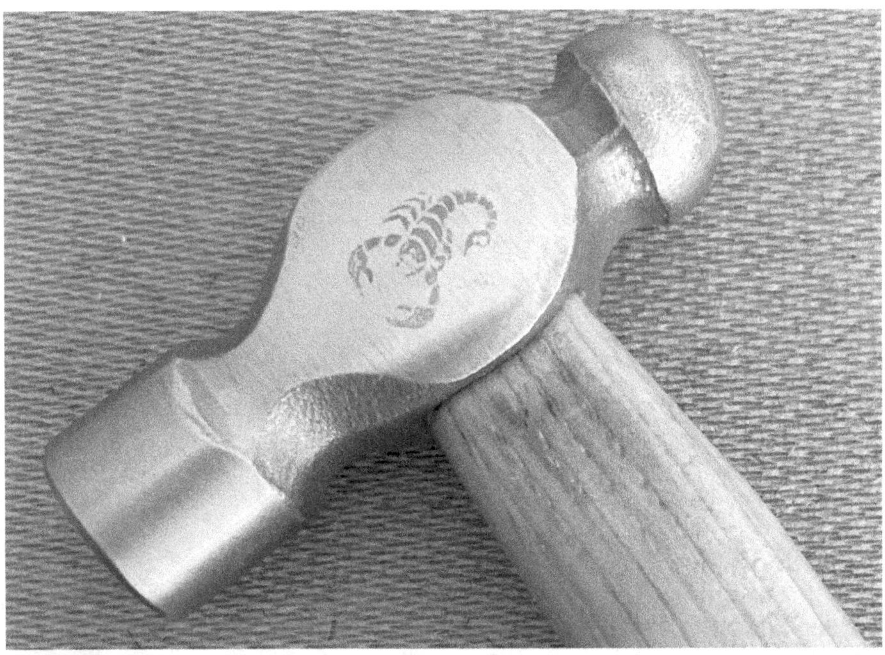

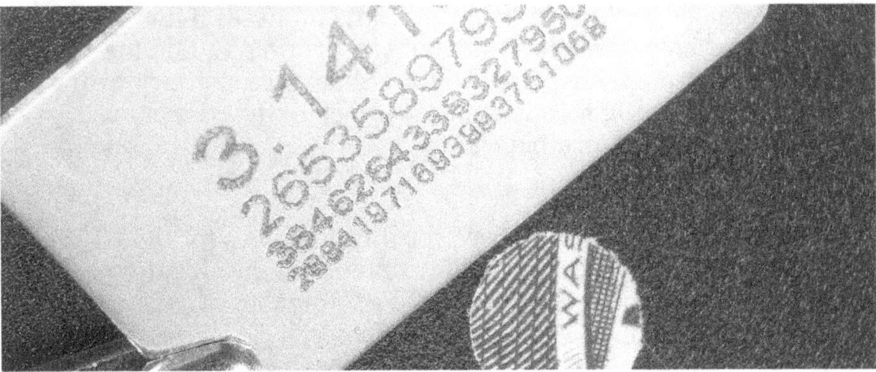

Chapter 2 - Make a Machine

How to Build an Electro Etch Machine

Make an etching machine with no electronics skill or soldering. Just a wire stripper or a pocket knife to remove insulation, and screw driver to assemble it. Look over the machine on the following page.

This electro etch machine will mark and etch using a low voltage power adapter. To choose an etch or a mark, just move an alligator clip between the MARK lug and ETCH lug. Just unclip and move it back and forth.

The ETCH lug is always DC and the MARK lug is always AC. We can safely move a clip back and forth bare handed because low voltage (less than 30V) is pretty safe. With dry hands, you won't notice the voltage. With wet hands use gloves. By moving a clip back and forth, we avoid soldering, drilling, switches, and a box.

This etching machine design uses stranded wire for the handpiece and workpiece wires, and solid wire for the etch lug and the mark lug that get the alligator clip.

Choosing Wire and a Wire Stripper

Stranded Wire
For the handpiece and workpiece wires, use 18AWG stranded wire - the size makes it easier to work with, and stranded wire is flexible. The 18 Gauge, 18AWG, and 18g are all the same. Some are not marked stranded, so look carefully at a cut end to see if it is solid or stranded. Any color. The next smaller size is 20AWG, and that's OK too. You can also use any wire you have that you can attach to an alligator clip. The 18g wire is easier to attach to the clip, but use anything you are comfortable with.

Solid Wire
A few inches of solid wire are used for the bare wires for the ETCH lug and MARK lugs. They are solid wire because the alligator clip chews up stranded wire. You only need a few inches of solid wire. If you buy a roll, the 18AWG solid is a useful size.

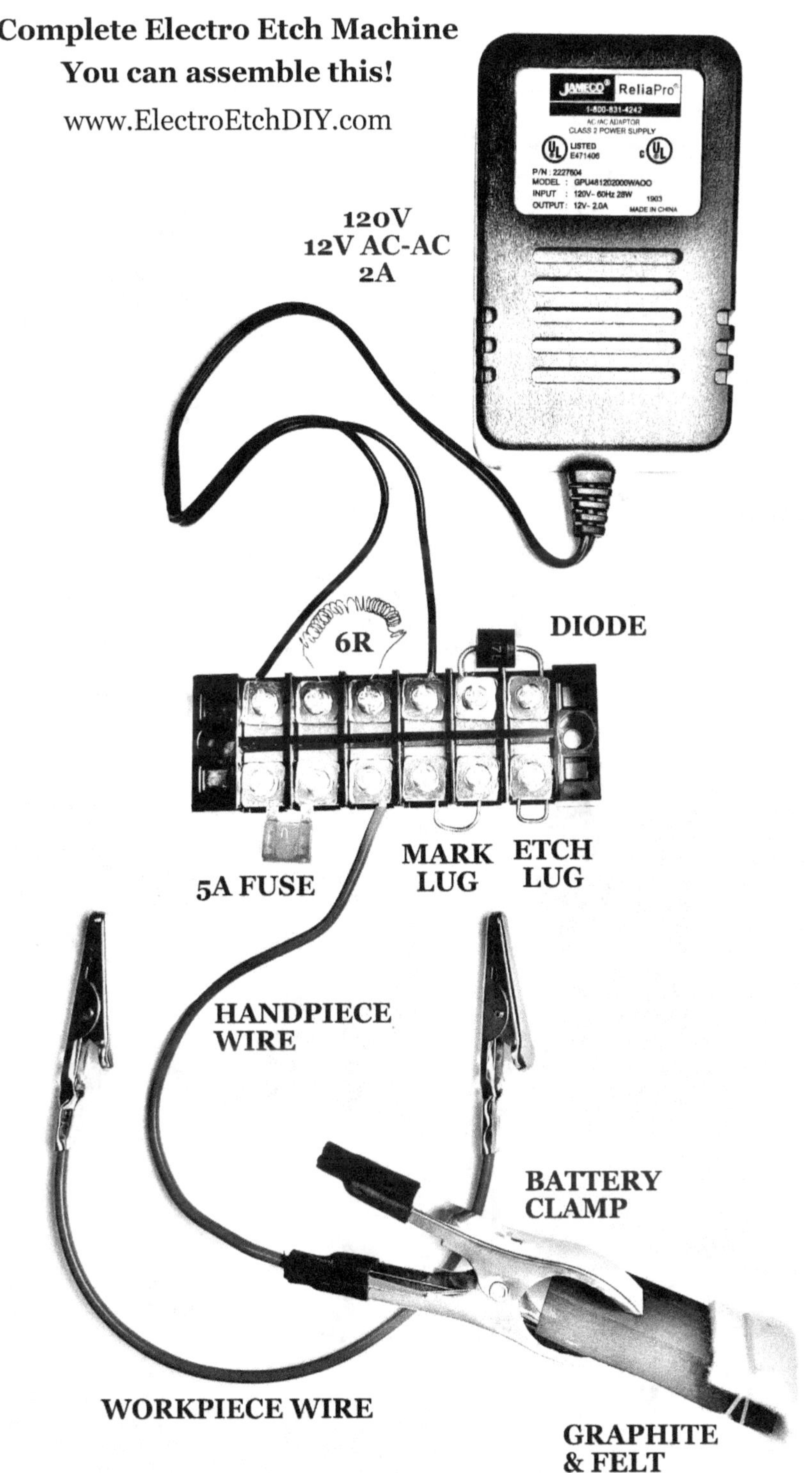
Complete Electro Etch Machine
You can assemble this!
www.ElectroEtchDIY.com
120V
12V AC-AC
2A
JAMECO ReliaPro
1-800-831-4242
AC /AC ADAPTOR
CLASS 2 POWER SUPPLY
UL LISTED
E471406
P/N : 2227604
MODEL : GPU481202000WAOO
INPUT : 120V- 60Hz 28W
OUTPUT : 12V- 2.0A
1903
MADE IN CHINA
6R
DIODE
MARK
LUG
ETCH
LUG
5A FUSE
HANDPIECE
WIRE
BATTERY
CLAMP
WORKPIECE WIRE
GRAPHITE
& FELT

MACHINE PARTS

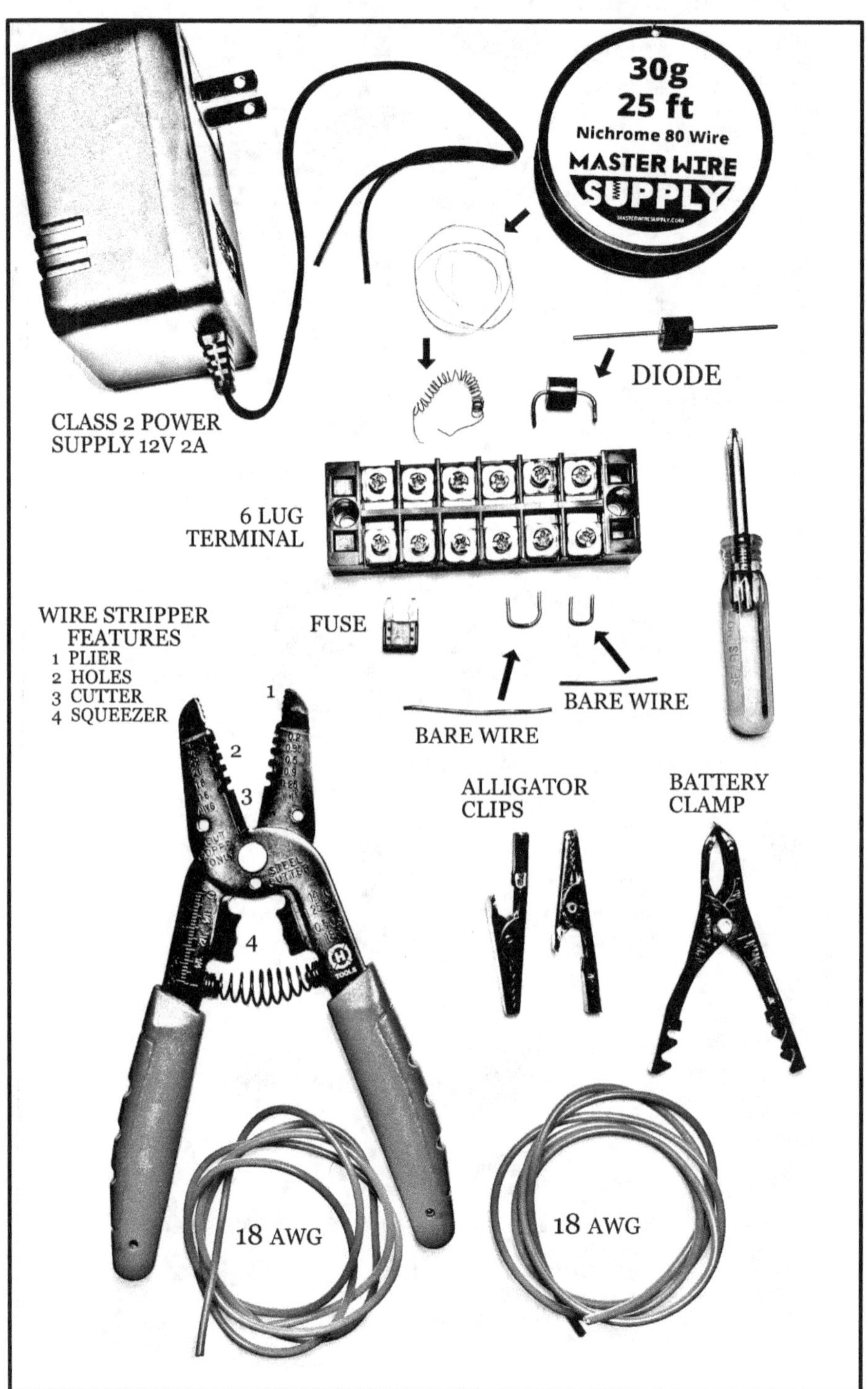

PARTS LIST

Each part is explained in detail along with how to find them, and the next chapter explains the handpiece, workpiece, and electrolytes.

Parts List For Electro Etch Machine
____ Stranded 18AWG Copper Wire (few feet), big box store
____ Solid Wire (few inches), salvage, or buy 18AWG
____ Assorted Alligator Clips and Clamps, Amazon, eBay
____ Heat Shrink or Tape for sharp edges
____ Terminal Block, 6 Lug, Milapeak brand, clamp style, 25A
____ Power Adapter 12V 2A, Jameco #2227604 / Triad WAU12-2000
____ Rectifier Diode, Jameco, 6A, 50V, #177754, or similar
____ Fuse 5A, Mini Blade, big box store or online
____ 12V 20W Halogen Bulb with pin legs, hardware store or online
____ or 11" of 30g Nichrome 80 wire
____ Wire Stripper, size 26-16AWG, Jameco 127862 or similar
____ Screwdriver (Phillips, for the terminal block)
____ Pliers of most any kind, or on the stripper
____ Switch Plug, big box store or hardware store, optional
____ Short Extension Cord, optional
____ Small Board to Mount on with screws or tape

Parts List For Handpiece and Electrolyte
____ Felt sheet material from the craft store
____ Graphite rod 3/8" online, or from a D carbon zinc battery
____ Graphite block 1" x 2" x 1/2" thick, on eBay
____ Base plate
____ White Vinegar 5% (found everywhere)
____ Salt and Baking Soda
____ Cleaning Ammonia
____ Bottles for Electrolyte
____ Rubber Bands
____ Tap water, Paper towels
____ Quart plastic bags work surfaces

Choosing a Base Plate for Etching Machine
The workpiece wire connects to the etching machine at the mark lug or the etch lug, and the other end connects to your tumbler or a base plate, a small metal sheet to set parts on that are hard to attach a clip to. Foil works but is not heavy enough; stainless steel is better. Bend a corner up to make a place for the alligator clip. On Amazon search "stainless steel sheet 26 gauge" and sort for price. Mine is 4" x 4".

Choosing a Wire Stripper

If you don't have a wire stripper, get the kind with a series of little holes; it should have a cutter, a tip that can grab, and a sorta-crimper that is for alligator clips.

How to Strip Wire

Removing insulation from the end of a wire with a tool is easy, but takes a little practice. These instructions are based on the style wire stripper with a series of small holes for the wire sizes. Find the hole in the stripper marked 18, then choose the next larger one. Put the wire in the hole about half an inch from the end of the wire, and close it down, move the stripper half way around the wire and back. Give it a push, and it's tough. Move to the 18 hole, and it works a lot better. Clip off the stripped wire, and practice several times. The insulation should slide off with a little push after the insulation is cut. Mainly learn to choose the hole and pull the insulation off without cutting lots of the wires or having to work very hard. Do several until it's easy to slide the insulation off.

Alligator Clips & Clamps

Search for "assorted electrical clamps" or "assorted alligator clips and battery clamps" for about $12 on Amazon and less at Harbor Freight. Attaching to alligator clips takes practice, and they rust, so having extras will come in handy. The larger clamps from the set will hold your handpiece graphite. If it will open enough to grip the handpiece, it will work. If you just need a larger clamp, it is called a Battery Clamp at $3 a pair at the big box.

About the Handpiece Wire and Workpiece Wire

Building an electro etch machine starts with two important parts. A handpiece wire and a workpiece wire. *The photos show short wires so they are easier to follow; your wires will be longer.*

The handpiece wire has a battery clamp on one end that will hold your graphite handpiece, and the other end is screwed down to your etching machine.

The workpiece wire has an alligator clip on both ends. One end will clip to your etching machine, and the other will clip to your base plate or the steel you are decorating.

Make the Workpiece Wire

Cut about 10" of the stranded wire and strip half an inch off each end, and fold the copper back over the insulation. Place it in the alligator clip with the wire-side against the metal to keep stragglers together, and carefully squeeze down the arms, or squeeze the tube to grip the wire, then do the other end. Tug to test. Tape or shrink wrap if sharp.

Make the Handpiece Wire

The handpiece wire has a clamp on one end that will hold a piece of graphite, and the other end is screwed to your machine. Cut about 16" of the stranded wire and strip half an inch off, and fold the copper back over the insulation, just like the workpiece wire. Feed the wire into the body of the clamp - around the pivot and spring - and back to the other arm. A "U" shape. Each arm of the clamp will grip wire. One arm will hold the stripped end; the other will hold insulated wire. Fold over the arm tabs on the stripped end, with the bare wire towards the metal. Fold over the arm tabs onto the insulation on the other arm, and make sure it's secure.

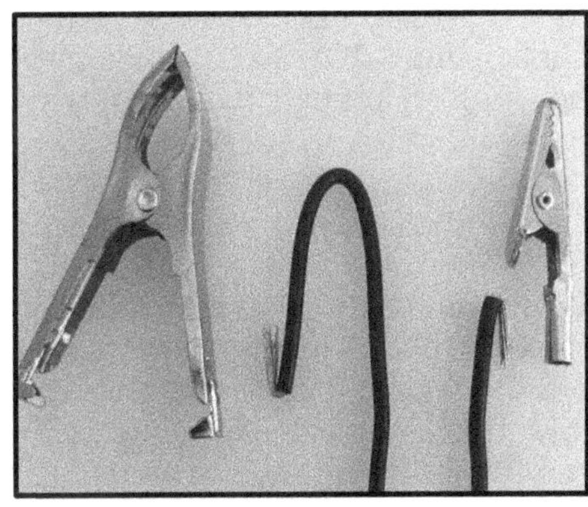

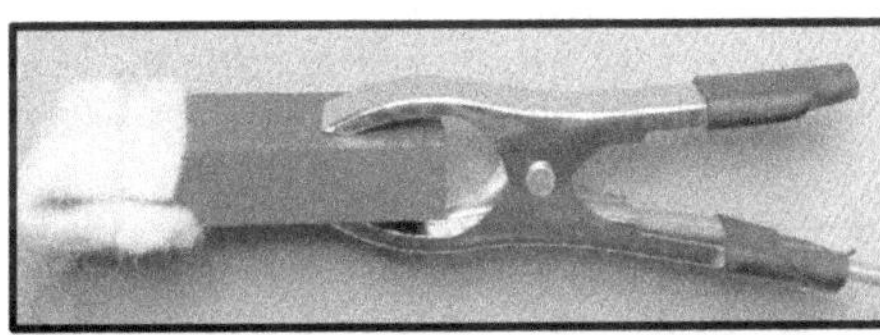

Tape or heat shrink the arms to protect your fingers from sharp edges. If you've done this before, use whatever method works.

Choosing a Terminal Block

This machine uses a 6 lug terminal block, and all the parts will clamp down. The kind to buy has a little plate that moves up and down like a clamp for each lug. Your wire goes *between the two plates* and when it's screwed down, it is a clamp, and makes it easy to attach things.

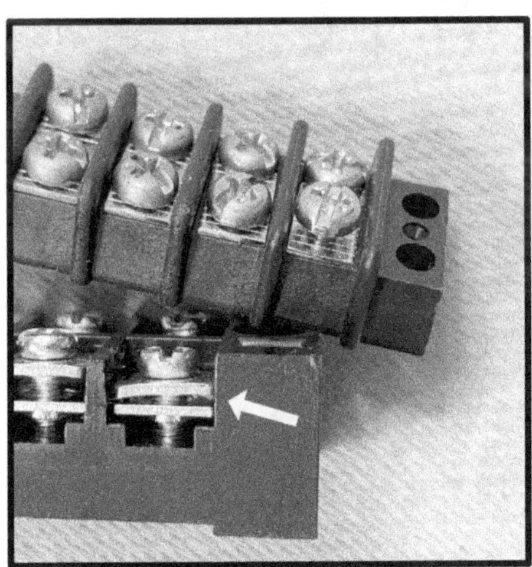

You can see the plates on the lower block in the photo. There are 15A and 25A versions and either will work, but the 25A is larger and easier to work with. If you are on Amazon, the brand Milapeak is the kind I like. Look for ones that are about three and half inches long (or 88mm). They come as a four-pack at about $15 with some other parts added in. Other brands are good if it has the clamp style lug. I have never seen the right kind at a big box store.

Buying a 12V AC-AC Power Adapter

An etching machine that will mark needs a low voltage AC-AC power adapter. It will be around $15 for the Jameco "12V 2A AC-AC Adapter", part number 2227604, or, if it is sold out, get the Triad WAU12-2000 12V 2A AC-AC adapter from Newark, Mouser, or Digikey for $18 or so. If you have an orphan adapter, see the chapter on using an adapter to see if it will work. A transformer is great too, but is more involved; see the chapter on using a transformer. This adapter has a 12V 2A transformer inside of it, and no, we don't cut open the case. For a 24V adapter, see the chapter on adapters.

When you buy an adapter online, get it from a reputable seller. Your fingers will be touching what is coming out of the adapter, and if it is not a safe one, it can hurt you. The online flea markets do not have any controls in place for counterfeit or faulty devices, and product safety markings may not be real. If there is a problem, the jumble name company will close and reopen with a new jumble name and some fake reviews. Look carefully at who the supplier is, and if they sell an adapter and fuzzy slippers and hair products, choose a different one. On Amazon, look for Jameco Reliapro 12VAC. Make sure you see a label on the product that says Class 2 Power Supply.

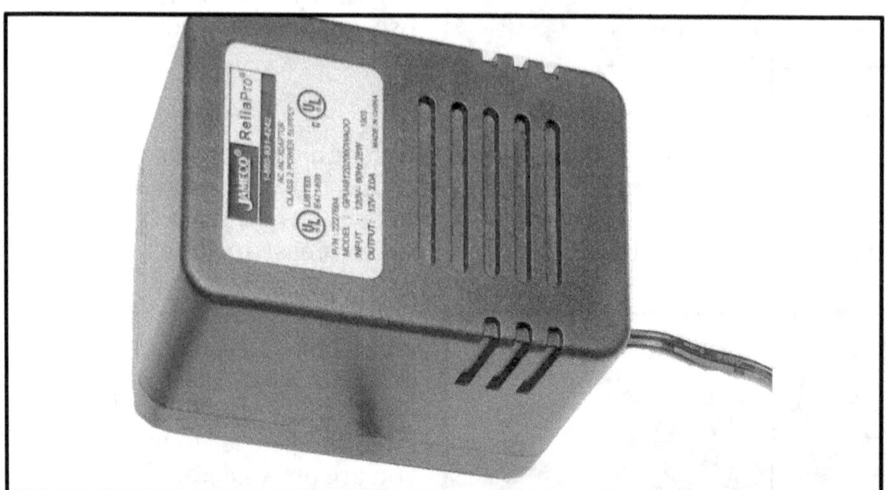

Choosing a Switch Plug or Wall Tap

An easy way to turn on and off an adapter is a wall plug with a switch and a light. Make *sure* it has a three prong or has a wide blade and narrow blade for safety, or off may not really be off. I use a short extension cord too. Having an ON light is worth hunting for.

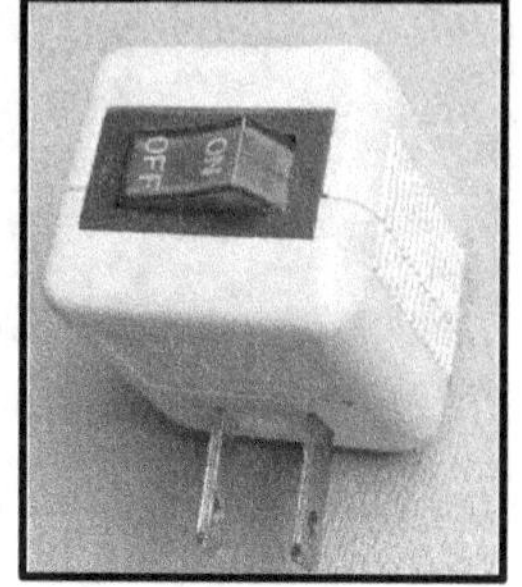

Choosing a Fuse
The fuse is attached into the terminal block. Use
a 5A blade fuse; it is tan or gold. Get a few in
case of mistakes; it is the small kind a car uses
and are marked ATC or ATM or Mini on the
package, and they are about 1/2" wide, or 3/4"
wide, and has legs.

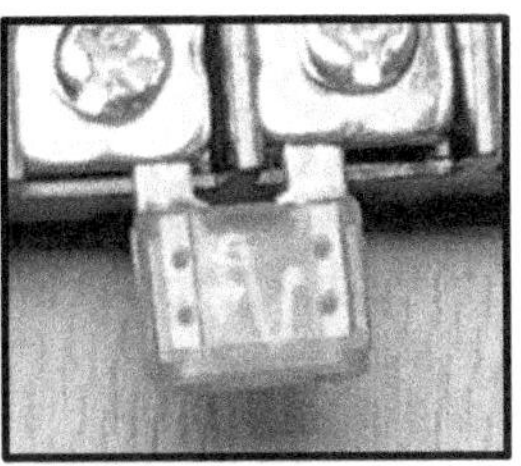

Choosing a Resistor
To be successful, your machine needs a way to control the power or
amps. An easy way to do this is with either a small halogen lightbulb,
or, a short length of special wire called Nichrome 80.

Choosing a Bulb as a Resistor
A small bulb that is 12V 20W Halogen with a Bi-Pin Base (two little
wire legs or pins) is about $7 for two. The bulb is nice because it
provides feedback while you work. Make sure it is 12V since it is
usually in tiny print, and 120V gets mixed in on the shelf. Don't worry
about all the other codes. You can use different power bulbs, like
10W, 20W, and 35W. When you insert the legs of the bulb to bridge
two lugs, tighten each lug *lightly* so the legs are aligned, then tighten.
If one is tightened down first, it can twist and shatter the glass when
the other one is tightened. The tiny shards fly and are invisible.

Don't use LED bulbs unless you want the low power they provide. At
some point the halogen bulbs may not be available, but Nichrome 80
wire resistors work as well or better, and are less expensive. You can
get a couple dozen resistors from a roll.

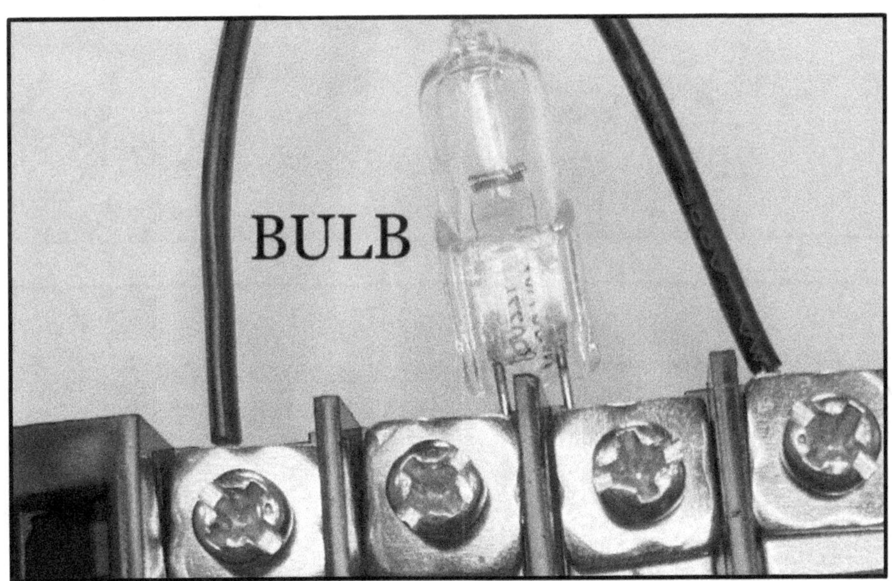

Choosing a Wire Resistor

Nichrome 80 wire makes a good resistor. Get a roll of wire for about $7, and make a 6R or 6 ohm resistor. Cut 11 inches of 30g Nichrome 80, and wind it on a thin rod or stick to turn it into a spring shape. Leave a leg on each end so it can be mounted on the terminal block (instead of the bulb), then bend it up a little so it's away from the other wires. The coils in the spring should not overlap, so spread them out a little. Use a piece of scrap wood under your machine while testing it, since if you use the wrong gauge wire, or too short a wire, or higher voltage, it can sag and burn the table. When you are testing the machine, the wire coils may get hot in one area and not the rest. Just let it cool, and separate the coils, then the heat should spread out. You can make a resistor for any voltage power source and amps using different wire gauges - see the chapter on resistors. When you insert the wire in the terminal block, make sure the plates catch it and hold. Sometimes I have to shift the wire and tighten again.

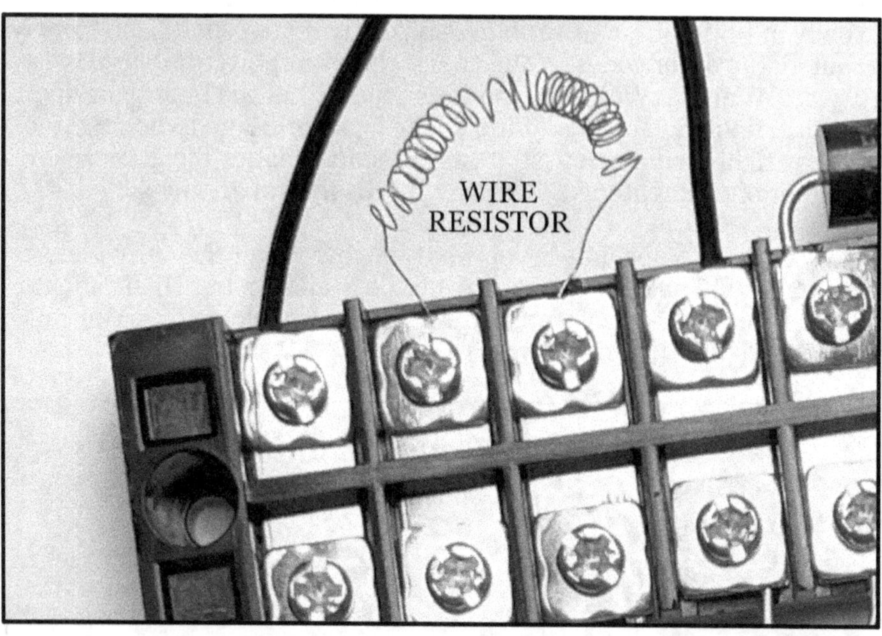

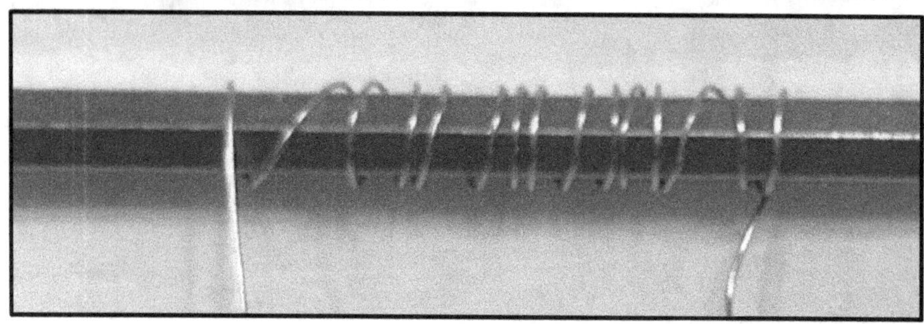

Choosing a Rectifier Diode

Don't let this little thing intimidate you. It is just a little barrel looking thing on a wire with a stripe on one end, and it produces the DC needed for etching. Get the Rectifier Diode, 6A, 50V, Jameco 177754, less than a $1. Make sure it looks something like the one in the picture and has a stripe on one end. If it is sold out, it's called a called a "silicon diode rectifier"; get one that is 4A or more, and 24V or more so it won't burn up. Many are out there. Bend the ends of the rectifier to a U shape that will bridge two lugs side by side, and trim so it fits. The 25A terminal block is shown.

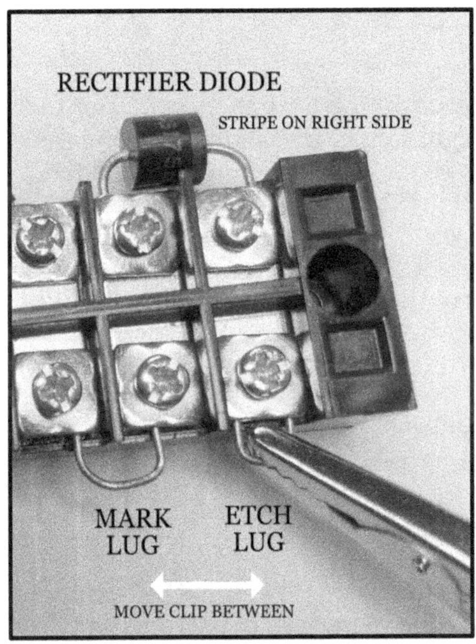

Move The Clip For Mark and Etch

Instead of soldering a toggle switch between DC and AC, just move the alligator clip between the ETCH and MARK bare wire lugs on the machine.

For the 12V power adapter (and other low less than 30 volts), it is safe to use your hands of they are dry; if your hands are wet, use gloves.

Buying Parts & Resources

See www.electroetchdiy.com for the latest recommended parts and where to buy them.

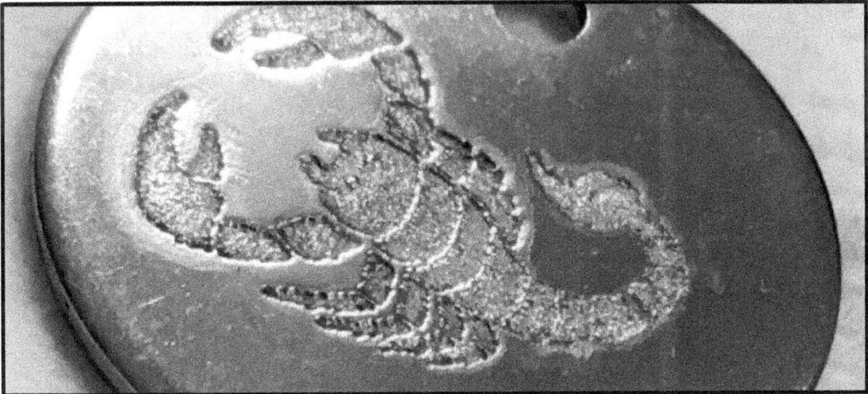

Assembly of Version 1

12V AC-AC Power Adapter
Cut the tip off the adapter output wire, and split the wire about 6",
then remove some insulation from the end of each wire.

Make the Bare Wires for the Mark Lug and Etch Lug
Make two bare solid wires, one 1" long, the other 1.5" long. Strip it,
then cut the wire. Bend the 1.5" to a U shape to bridge two lugs. This
will be for the MARK lug. Bend the 1" wire for the ETCH lug; it goes
into just one lug.

Assemble the Wires
See the layout of all the parts in place on the next page, and refer to
the large complete layout at the beginning of the chapter. Laying the
terminal block in front of you with the 6 lugs going left to right, the
Back lugs are on the far side, Front lugs are on the closer side.

Back #1 - attach one of the Power Adapter wires. Either one.
Back #2 and #3 - insert the legs of the bulb or wire resistor.
Back #4 - attach the other Power Adapter wire.
Back #5 and #6 - attach Diode, the stripe to the right.

Front #1 and #2 - insert the Fuse legs.
Front #3 - attach your Handpiece Wire.
Front #4 and #5 - insert Bare wire (1.5") the MARK LUG.
Front #6 - insert Bare wire (1") in the lug, the ETCH LUG.

If your resistor is a thin wire, make sure to position it in the terminal
block so it catches. Sometimes the little plates aren't flat, and don't
grab a thin resistor wire so shift it a little to make it catch. If using a
bulb, gently tighten each leg, then tighten.

Testing the Machine
Separate the handpiece clamp, and the workpiece clip so they aren't
touching anything. Turn on the power adapter. There should be no
light from the bulb or heat on the resistor wire, and no other activity.
If the fuse blows, unplug and go over things carefully.

Move the workpiece alligator clip to the bare wire at Front #6 for
ETCH, and touch the handpiece and workpiece ends. The bulb will
light up or the resistor wire will get hot. That's correct.

Now move the workpiece alligator clip to the bare wire at #4 & #5 for
MARK, and touch the handpiece and workpiece ends again. The bulb
will light up again or the resistor wire will get hot. That's correct.

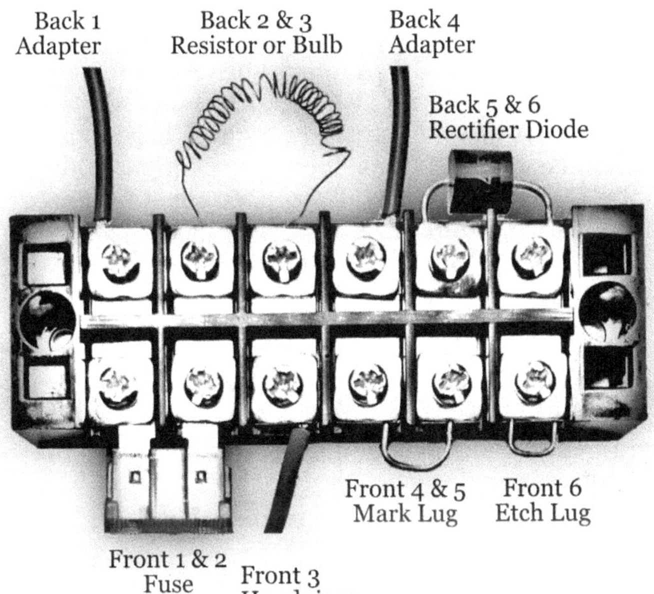

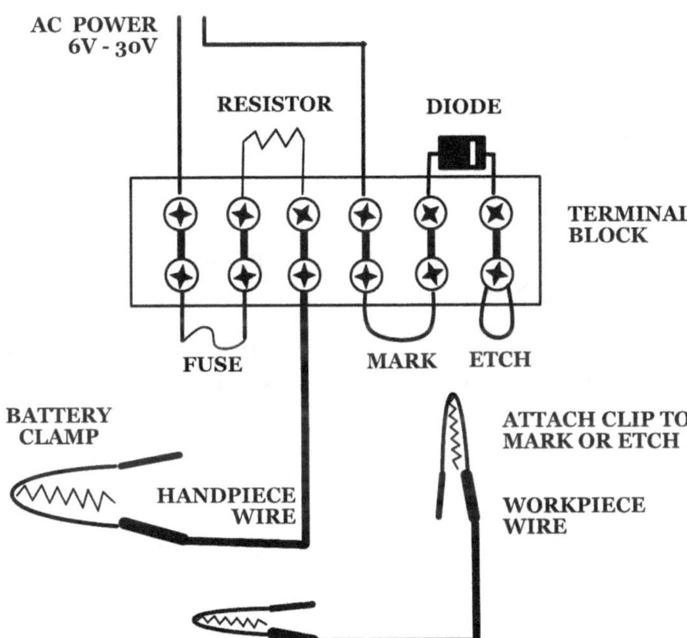

Skip to the Handpiece Chapter

Time to skip to the chapter on making a handpiece, or read on for using batteries, transformers and other adapters.

Assembly of Version 2

Version 2 works with a battery, a DC adapter, a bench power supply, or retrofitting your machine. You can also use an AC source for a machine that just marks. Assembly may require more tools, since there are different kinds of connections, including clamps, soldering, crimping, or adapters. The Version 2 will work for any power source between 3V and 30V with a different resistor. See the chapter on resistors.

More Parts
____ Terminal Block, 4 Lugs
____ Wire 18g solid
____ Clips and Connectors
____ Resistor for the Volts and Amps
____ Fuse for the Amps Needed

Choosing a Power Source
See the chapters on choosing a battery or an adapter. Select a resistor from the resistor chapter that works for the voltage and amps.

Connecting With Solid Wire
Connecting to a battery or existing machine may be better with 18g solid wire so the terminal block will stay put. *Always connect the battery last.*

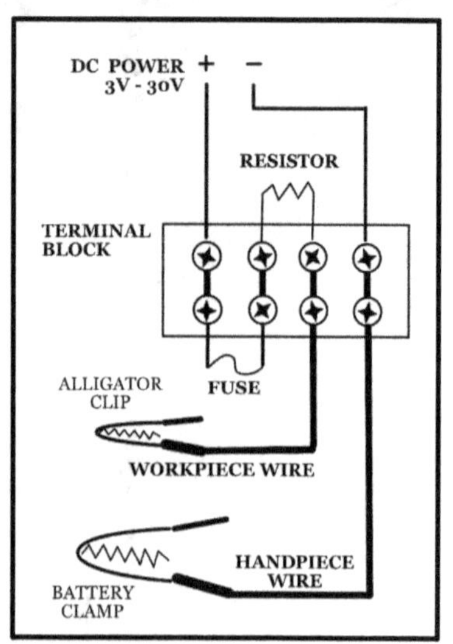

Assembly
Laying the terminal block in front of you with the lugs going left to right, the back lugs are on the far side, front lugs the closer side.

You will only use four lugs, and the arrangement is different than Version 1. The workpiece wire only needs one alligator clip to connect to the base plate. If your resistor is a thin wire, make sure to position it in the terminal block so it catches. Sometimes the little plates aren't flat, and don't grab a thin resistor wire.

Back #1 - attach the positive **+** lead from the power source.
Back #2 and #3 - insert the resistor wire or bulb.
Back #4 - attach the negative lead from the power source.

Front #1 and #2 - insert the Fuse legs.
Front #3 - attach your Workpiece wire here.
Front #4 - attach your Handpiece wire here.

AA Battery Etching Machine

This machine is using two AA batteries. They are 1.5V in series so they provide 3V - enough to etch. You can use AAA, C, or D sizes, and lithium, carbon zinc, or alkaline. The nickel cadmium are only 1.2V, so use three of them.

There is a little extra space in the battery holder so the battery can be removed without tearing the wrapper. Find a holder with a picture showing batteries in it (some have a switch and cover and are not as tight).

The 1.5R resistor is 11" of 24g Nichrome 80 and will limit power to two amps and 6 watts. With four batteries (6V), the same resistor works, and will give you 4A and 24 watts.

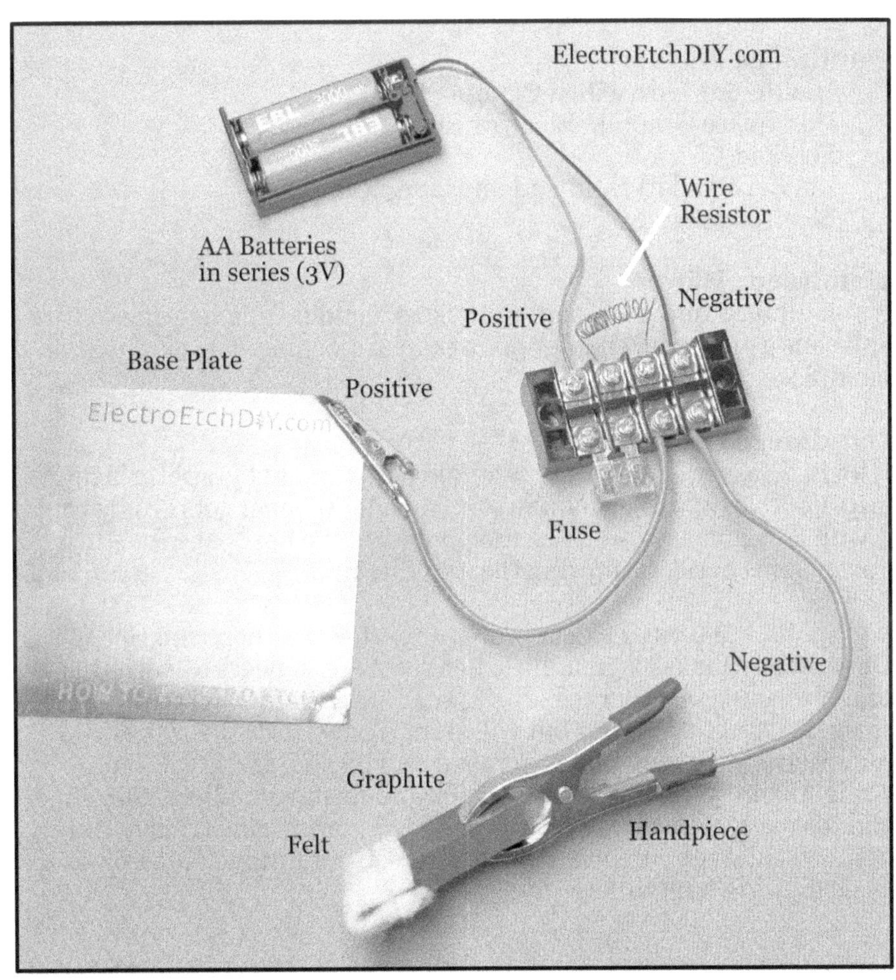

Chapter 3 - Make a Handpiece

Handpiece, Pads, and Electrolytes

The working end of an electro etch machine is a handpiece with a wet pad dabbed all over the stencil, and etching or marking. It transfers electricity and electrolyte to the surface, hopefully only where your stencil allows it, and picks up oxides from the steel.

This chapter will show you how to make a handpiece, choose pads, and make electrolyte and neutralizer.

Handpiece Parts
____Handpiece Wire with a Clamp
____Handpiece Graphite Block or Rod
____Felt Pad
____Rubber Band to Hold Pad on Handpiece
____Electrolyte

Handpiece Wire
If you jumped into this chapter, the instructions for a handpiece wire and clamp are in the chapter on making a machine. The clamp grips a handpiece.

Handpiece Graphite for $1
A lot of different handpiece materials will work, but graphite is my favorite. It is easy to get, and won't corrode. When it gets crusty wipe it with a wet paper towel. See the photos on the next page for a teardown of a D battery, showing the graphite rod.

A graphite rod from inside a D or C or even AA carbon zinc Heavy Duty battery makes a great little handpiece. Use pliers to peel back the top crimped lid on the battery. Tear it up over a safe work surface since the stuff that comes out will stain. You will see the rod as you remove the gooey top plates of metal and plastic, and it will pull straight out if you twist it gently back and forth with pliers. Clean it, and it's ready. The dollar type stores carry carbon zinc (Heavy Duty) batteries, and they are available online. Do not open alkaline batteries since they are built differently.

Graphite Blocks and Rods

Graphite rods and blocks are available online. My favorite graphite blocks are on eBay from Saturn Industries. I use a 1/2" or 3/8" thick block that is a couple of inches long and an inch wide. There are different grades and they don't matter - just the size and cost. It should cost less than $15 after shipping. You can also get a larger one and cut it down with a coarse saw, then square it off with sandpaper so it has an even face; cutting the block is no fun.

Drilling Graphite

The graphite is easy to drill, and adding a bolt with a wire connector looks nice - until the bolt corrodes and the wire turns green. The different bolts I tried did not last, and I moved to using the clamp after the 3rd eaten up bolt.

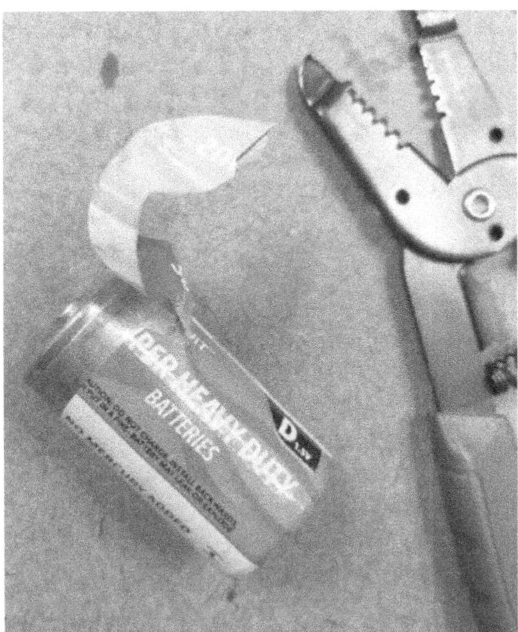

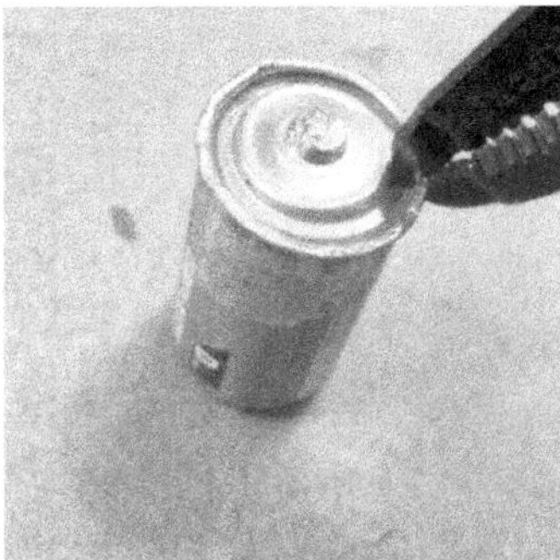

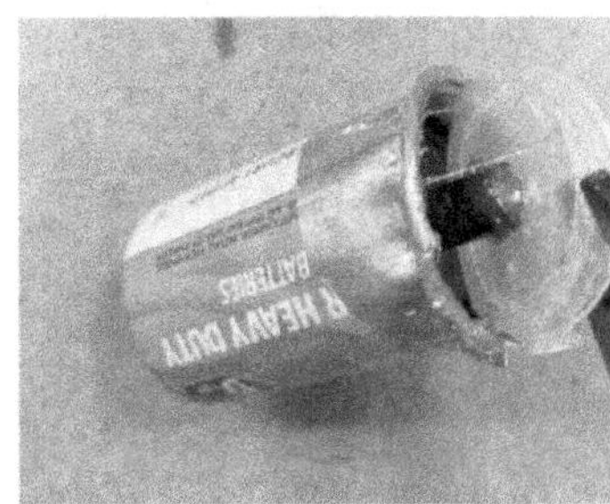

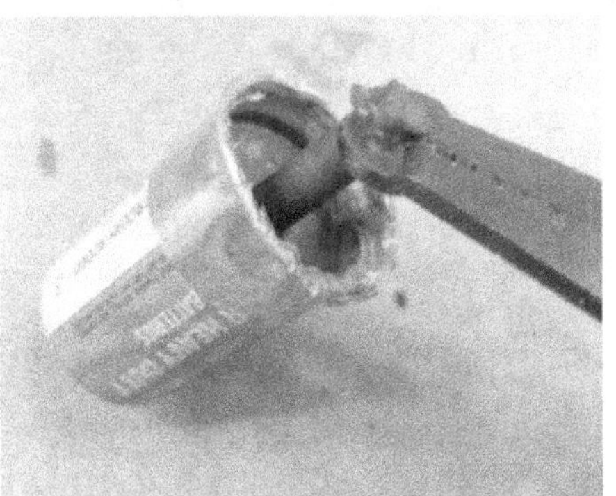

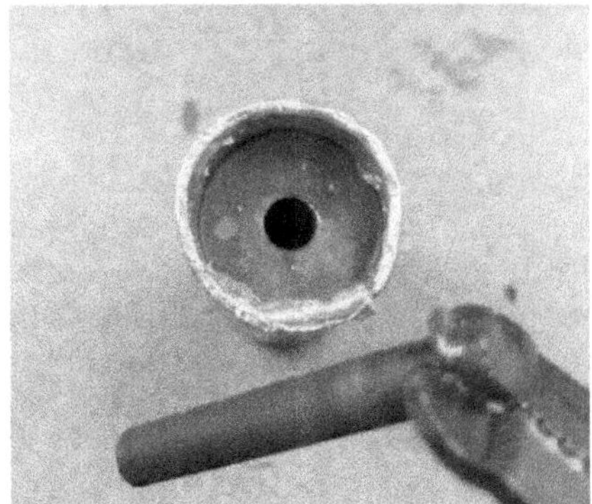

Handpiece Insulation - Electrical / Heat

With a clamp holding your handpiece and a resistor controlling the amps, the heat is controlled, and it's low voltage. If you don't control the amps, your handpiece may get hot. On a long etch it will warm up, but should not get too hot.

Handpiece Should Have a Flat Surface

The etching and marking process is picky about the distance between the handpiece surface and the surface of the metal you are decorating. If the handpiece is not even/flat under the pad, it will cause some differences in the mark or etch. Flatten the graphite with sandpaper on a flat surface, and use a rolling motion on curves.

All About Electro Etching Pads

A pad is attached to your handpiece then moistened with electrolyte. It passes electricity through your stencil, and takes in the oxides. A lot of different things work as a pad, but there is are differences between a pad for a mark and for an etch.

Pads for Marking

The pad for marking can be thin or thick. I've used felt, t-shirt, makeup pads, denim, disposable shop towels, ... lots of things work. A pad used for marking can be used several times.

Pads for Etching

The pad for etching works better if it is thicker. Double it up if needed. It holds the oxides from the etch and holds more electrolyte. You may only get one etch or part of an etch from a pad before it gunks up depending on the artwork, the metal, and the thickness of the pad and the amps, but thicker is better. The idea is to soak up the oxide gunk from an etch and hold it, and stay wet during the process. Lots of materials work for this. The craft felt pad is what I've settled on.

During an etch, metal oxides are being pushed from your steel through the stencil and into your pad, and a felt pad holds more of it along with staying wet. Don't rinse pads, they have lots of metals.

Choosing Felt

Big box stores with a craft aisle should have felt sheets. The thicker the felt the better. Don't use real wool felt since it has oils that keep it from wetting. The pads I get will wet as soon as the surface tension breaks on the drops. The felt is in lots of colors and sold by the square foot or larger. I cut it into little pieces, and use it for both etching and marking. They work well as little polishing pads.

Attaching the Pad
Cut the felt (or material) into pieces that you can wrap on the end of your handpiece, and hold it with a small rubber band. It should cover the whole end.

Electrolyte
An electrolyte is a salt solution that passes between the metal surface and handpiece pad, carrying electricity and metal oxides. The electro etch supply companies sell electrolyte they have developed with lot of research and testing. Their recipes are a secret, but they are experts with special metals that go into airplanes, rockets, medical devices, and knives. If you call them, and explain what kind of metal you are having trouble with, they have probably solved that problem. Some stores allow online ordering and some require a phone call. Check on the shipping cost before you get too far, at least so you'll know. Ask about any special safety rules for the products they suggest, and about neutralizer requirements.

Making Electrolyte
There are hundreds of "it works for me" stories on the internet, and hundreds more of "it does not work for me". Hopefully, these recipes and instructions will get you to 99.44 percent success. You can make or buy an electrolyte that will work for most things. There are some more complicated home brew recipes, but the parts cost more than commercial electrolyte.

Electro Etch Electrolyte Bottles
Use plastic bottles with a dispenser cap of some sort, and a piece of tape on it with the mix written on it.

Types of Salt for Electrolyte
Use coarse table salt to match the recipe, or fine salt or iodized table salt. My tests show they all work. I use coarse salt. If you use fine salt, maybe use a little bit less, or measure it if you have a scale. The coarse salt measure of ¾ tsp is about 4 grams.

Vinegar for Electrolyte
The most common white vinegar is 5% acidic and works well for lots of etching and marking. I tried other concentrations and settled on 5% from the grocery store.

Baking Soda
Use regular grocery store baking soda.

Water for Electrolyte
Distilled water might give you more consistent results but tap water is usually fine. Some water is soft, some is hard. Stir for a few seconds.

Electrolyte Recipes
These won't work for everything, but they are tested on lots of steels. One version might work better than the other for the steel or stencil. Sometimes the difference is a mark that is slightly browner or blacker or grayer. In the recipes, a tsp is a teaspoon, or 5 ml. The recipes here are safe and work almost all the time. For factory or production etching and marking, the commercial versions may work better.

Electrolyte Recipes

Recipe 1 "saltwater and vinegar"
3/4 tsp coarse salt (4g)
2 tsp white vinegar 5% acidic (common)
8 oz water - distilled might be a good idea
pH is about 3

Recipe 2 "saltwater and baking soda"
3/4 tsp coarse salt (4g)
1 tsp baking soda
8 oz water - distilled might be a good idea
pH is about 8

Recipe 3 "saltwater"
3/4 tsp coarse salt (4g)
8 oz water

Neutralizer
2 tsp household ammonia
2 oz water
pH is about 10

Just saltwater will mark most tumblers but not all steels. Sometimes a mark with only saltwater wipes off with 12V, but works at 24V.

I use saltwater and vinegar for shallow/normal etching, and saltwater baking soda for deeper etching and some steels. If you don't get good results, you probably need a store bought electrolyte.

I mix the electrolyte solution in a larger container, then pour it into small bottles just to make them easier to keep organized. A little piece of tape tells me what is inside.

I use the same size bottle for my WD-40 or 3-in-One oil.
Wetting the pad, sometimes the electrolyte won't sink in until the surface tension breaks on the droplet. Saturate it until it almost drips.

Deeper Etching vs Normal Etching
For deeper etches, the baking soda is better. It does not deposit as much oxide on the steel during longer deeper etching. For marking, it is about the same as saltwater vinegar, but on most steels, I like the mark from saltwater vinegar better than baking soda.

If these don't work, call one of the electro etch companies and order from them. Some have a cross reference for electrolytes and dozens of metals. Some sell custom stencils, screen stencil film, thermal stencils, machines, and supplies, and some are very helpful. See my website www.ElectroEtchDIY.com for a list.

Test Your Steel with Electrolyte
Test your steel with the electrolyte you plan to use. In the chapter on etching, the test stencil is just Scotch blue painters tape with a hole punched in it from a paper punch. It makes a great test stencil, and you know pretty quick if things are working or not.

Salt Concentration
The amount of salt in your electrolyte makes a difference. I used to use more salt in my mix, but found that extra salt makes the etched surface quite a bit rougher.

Vinegar Concentration
I compared using just vinegar and salt vs the vinegar, salt and water, the recipe with vinegar and water worked better.

Skip to the stencils section to get your stencils, or to the etch section to make your first etch and mark.

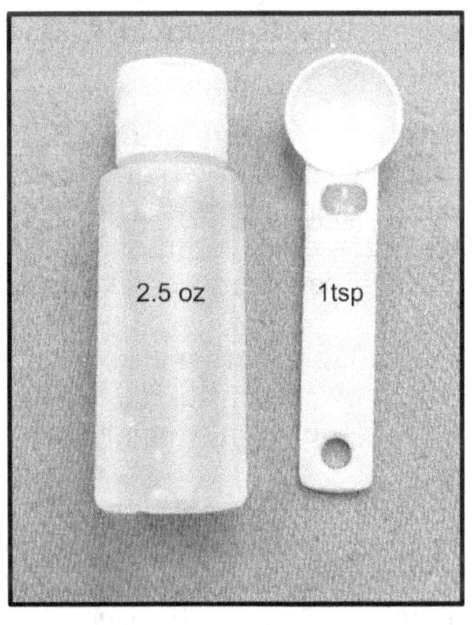

Adapters, Transformers, and Batteries
The next set of chapters explain how to choose an adapter, a transformer, different batteries, a DC bench supply, or retrofit a machine you already use. They can get a little more involved, and some builds require more tools and parts.

Resistors
There is also a chapter on making a resistor for any etching machine for any power source below 30V.

Chapter 4 - Adapters
Using an Adapter For an Etching Machine

This chapter explains how to use a thrift store or orphan power adapter from your box of electronics. A power adapter is the chunky boxy thing that hogs space on an outlet; also called a wall wart. The recommended machine uses one that is 12V 2A and AC out. There are lots of different voltages, sizes, AC-out or DC-out, and two kinds: Light and Heavy (weight). This chapter is about the kinds you might have already, buy, or find at the thrift shop. Some adapters are not safe because they can leak dangerous voltage, either immediately, or as they age.

Adapter Voltage and Amps
Adapters are marked different ways, so "1A" and "1000mA" are the same thing, and 24W is just 12V at 2A (volts * amps). The kind for DC are much more common than AC, and a DC adapter will etch, so it is useful if you want to make an etch-only Version 2 machine.

Most adapters are marked so you know if it is AC or DC, but some only show a bar with dashes under it, then the amps. That's DC. For AC out, there is a squiggly bar, then the amps it produces.

You can sort the adapters with your eyes closed. The ones that might be good are cube shaped and heavy. It should also be at least 6V, if it is AC out. If you have a big heavy ones with screw terminals that old phones and doorbells used - those are good too.

Good Adapter Features
If you find a heavy one, look at the markings for these features:

    1. Just one voltage out. It might be 6V, 9V, 12V, 14V, 18V,...

    2. Says "Class 2" then some other words

    3. It is heavy and cube shaped.

    4. If it is AC and more than 6V out, or DC out more than 3V.

    5. It produces at least half an amp for the lower voltages

Power Adapters
Use Class 2

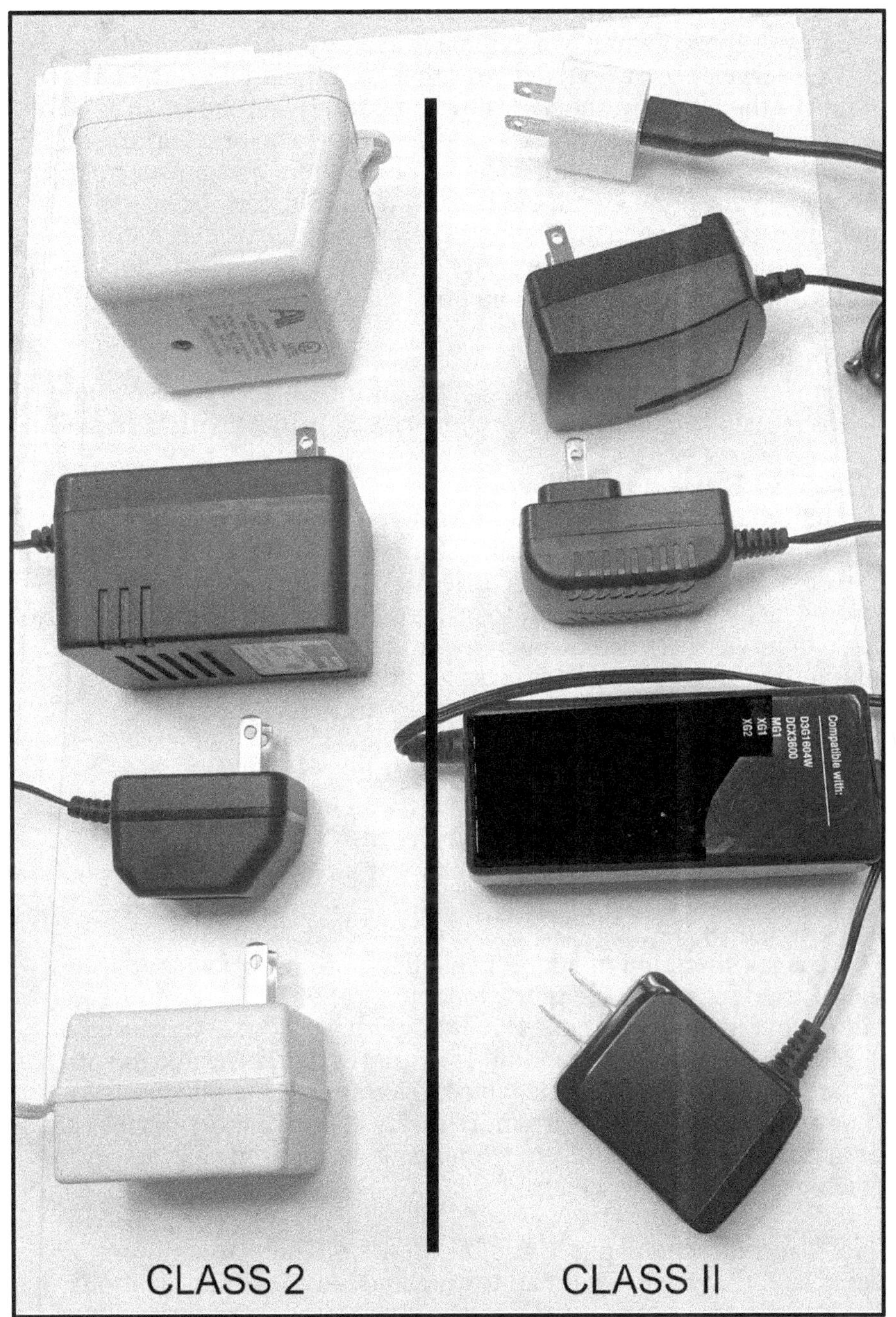

About "Class 2"

Most power adapters are designed to plug into a plastic box with no exposed wires. Your radio, router, or record player. Rarely does the electricity from the cord reach your fingers unless you are touching the tip, and many adapters hide the electrical contacts in the tip so you don't touch them by accident. We aren't plugging into a box, all safe from exposed wires, you will be touching what comes out, just like the service tech who fixed your thermostat, and used to fix the phone in the alcove in the hall (now you know what those wires were for). A service tech always tests the wire voltage before working on it. Sometimes even with a multimeter. The adapters that power many of those low voltage AC hands-on wires have a transformer inside, making it cube shaped and heavy. They usually say "Class 2 Power Supply" or something similar. The transformer gives you a lot of protection from high voltage and don't depend on lots of parts.

Shopping For "Class 2"

When you search online for class 2 transformers both "Class 2" and "Class II" will be listed. Some are incorrectly printed with "Class 2".

Where to Buy Adapters

Buy online from an electronics store if you don't find a good one at home or a thrift store. Electronics stores actually care about this stuff, and do not source from bad factories or jumble name companies formed last week. If you need to, call and order from the online store, since their websites can be overwhelming, say "I need a 12V power adapter that is 2 amps and is class 2, the number 2". If you order an adapter but it's lightweight, return it. It has to feel solid.

Buying a 24V AC-AC Class 2 Adapter

The suggested machine uses 12V, but if you need 24V for the additional power, get a Jameco 24V 2A adapter is #2197548 or #2271119, or the Triad WAU24-1800. Use a resistor for 24V.

About "Class II"

There is another kind of adapter called a "switching power adapter" that is used for phone chargers, modems, routers, radios, and a million other things that use DC. It might have "Class II" printed on it. Most of the new kind are double insulated, and have a logo with a square inside a square. Some have the letters "LPS" that stands for "Limited Power Source" with more safety. Some of these devices have smarts that will prevent them from being used for an etching machine, but many will etch.

I don't recommend using "Class II" adapters. There are millions being sold that have never had testing and have fake certifications.

They might be printed with all the right things, and many of them will work for a while, but as they age, may not be safe. There are lots of videos showing the guts of poorly made adapters. Some can electrocute you from the git go, some can sneak up on you. The legit ones are designed safely, though there have been recalls.

USB Adapters

The phone and gadget chargers are also switching power adapters, and have a flat USB-A port. They are 5V DC and anywhere from .5A to 3A. They will etch, but be super careful, since there are millions of counterfeit or factory rejects that are dangerous and widely sold, and can leak 120V. There are millions of results for the search "my phone charger zapped me". It's almost never from a legit unit.

Resistor for Adapter

Every etching machine needs a resistor, so once you have a power adapter, it is time to match it up with a resistor. Your adapter will have the voltage and the rated amps printed on it. Use them to choose a resistor that will limit things to the rated amps for the voltage. The chapter on resistors lists several voltage and amps combinations, and how to make the resistor and burn it in.

Amp Ratings for Adapter

Most adapters are rated in round numbers, and there is some give in the ratings. The amps rating are on the safe side and assume full time use. You can use a resistor that pulls a bit more than the rating, and it still prevents a short at the end of the etching or marking process. Stencils work better without extra heat, so even if your power source handles several amps, using all of it will make things hot.

Installing an Adapter

Any DC power source from 3V to 30V, works with the Version 2 design with the right resistor and fuse. There are barrel plugs you can get if you don't want to clip the end off an adapter you use for something else.

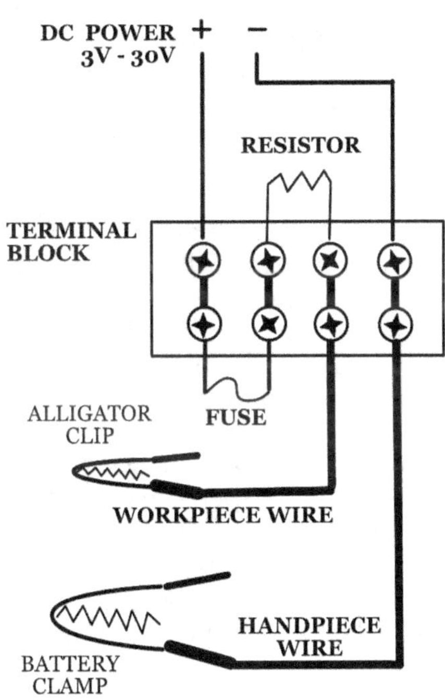

Chapter 5 - Transformers

Using a Transformer
for an Etching Machine

The cube shaped heavy electronic part inside a Class 2 adapter that
turns 120V into 12V is called a transformer. They are very good at
keeping the 120V side from the 12V side, and a transformer is inside
the recommended adapters. They are used with doorbells,
thermostats, telephones, and billions of other devices.

Why Use a Transformer

A transformer offers more choices than adapters, and adds a nice
retro vibe to your etching machine. If you use a recommended one, it
is easy to wire, but must be connected up properly.

Safety - Watch the Kids

Don't let kids handle a transformer without supervision. It has 120V
on one side, and it uses tape and varnish over copper coils to insulate
it, so if it is poked with fingers or a screwdriver, it is dangerous. A
healthy transformer is very safe (except from being poked at). If it's
all beaten up and dented, or old and crusty, don't use it. If you see
wire on the primary that is just varnished (you see the copper), put
some tape over it.

Safety - Unplug the Transformer

Unplug from the wall socket before you work on the connections to
the transformer. Just because a switch is off, it's not a guarantee that
there is no power going through the wires. The 12V side is very safe,
but the 120V side can kill you. Off is a relative thing, just assume the
cord is always hot, and unplug it when you are working it.

Safety - Get a Multimeter

Invest in an inexpensive ($10) multimeter to measure volts and
resistance, and watch some videos on how to use it. It will measure
volts and ohms. If that sounds complicated, just use an adapter
instead of a transformer. The measured DC volts on the ETCH lug
will be half the expected voltage on a multimeter, because of the
diode.

About Transformers

Transformers come in all sizes from tiny to huge, and are always AC-in and AC-out, even if it doesn't say, and they generally don't say, they just assume you know already. It takes in one AC voltage, and puts out a lower / higher / same AC voltage. For an etching machine, it will always lower the voltage. From 120V to 12V, or whatever, and it is called a "step down" transformer.

Line Voltage

To keep things simple, I will use 120V for the in-voltage, and 12V for the out-voltage to the etching machine. A transformer datasheet may say 110V, or 115V, or 117V, or 120V, and all will work fine as long as the output is low voltage.

About Amps and Transformers

The amp rating for a transformer is always for the output side; a 12V 2A transformer is rated for 2A at 12V, or 24 watts, or 24VA. The amp rating assumes continuous use at that amperage. Some transformers have an overload gadget and will stop for a little while or forever if you pull more than it's rating. Some don't, and will heat up till it smokes if more amps are pulled than it is designed for, plus your stencil and handpiece will get hot. Use a resistor, and don't smoke a transformer.

The recommended transformers listed below have only two wires going to the plug (120V), and two wires to the etching machine (12V or 24V). Buy your transformer online, or salvage it if it has markings so you can identify it. It should not look like it was underwater or crusty.

Buying a Transformer

____ jameco.com part 221356 12V 4A
____ digikey.com part 237-1938-ND for Triad F-219X, 12V 4A
____ mouser.com part 553-F219X for Triad F-219X, 12V 4A
____ newark.com part 51Y4833 for Triad F-219X, 12V 4A
____ Triad F-218X is 12V 2A
____ Triad F-229X is 24V 2A

Cord, Connectors & Fuse

____ Lamp Cord, with two prong, one larger
____ WAGO 221-412 Lever Connectors
____ Inline Blade Fuse Holder, with 16g wire or 18g wire leads
____ Blade Fuse 5A that fits in the inline fuse holder
____ Resistor Nichrome 80

Resistor
A transformer is designed for a voltage and amps (like 12V 2A) so choose a resistor that will limit things to the voltage and amps it will be happy with. The chapter on resistors lists several voltage and amps combinations, and how to make the resistor.

Choosing a Fuse Holder
Get an "Inline Blade Fuse Holder", and 5A fuses that will fit in it. The example here is ATM mini. See the photos. Some big box stores carry these, or get one online. Buy one with wire leads of 18g or 16g, since some have 12g or 14g and are very thick.

Choosing a Lamp Cord
A plug will go from your wall to the transformer. Salvage a two prong cord that has a wide blade and a narrow blade. The narrow blade is the "hot" side and it's insulation is smooth and will get the fuse. The other side of the cord will have lines molded into it.

Connecting a Lamp Cord
Wiring a 120V plug to a transformer is not hard, but it has to be done safely. Instead of wire nuts, tape, or crimps, I like the "WAGO 221-412" lever connector; the connections are side by side, but it will handle the wire sizes wires for lamp cords and transformers. Strip wire to 11mm and insert all the way in, then close the lever, and give it a tug. There is a handy line printed on the connector to check the stripped length. Once you clamp it down, it is very secure, and no copper should show outside the connector. The WAGO 221-412 are available online and at hardware stores for $6/10.

Wire the Lamp Cord to Fuse
Split the lamp cord and connect the "hot/smooth" wire to one of the fuse holder wires using a WAGO. See the picture on the next page.

Transformer Primary
There are two sides to a transformer, usually on either side of a block of steel plates. The "primary" side connects to 120V, and the "secondary" is low voltage and connects to your etching machine. There should be a datasheet that shows which side is the primary. If you can't find how it should be connected, don't do it.

Connecting the Transformer Primary
Using WAGO connectors, connect the lamp cord wire and fuse wire to the leads on the *primary* side of the transformer. The lamp cord MUST be on the primary side or there are sparks when it's plugged in. If you aren't 100% sure which side should have the 120V, don't attach the lamp cord to the transformer.

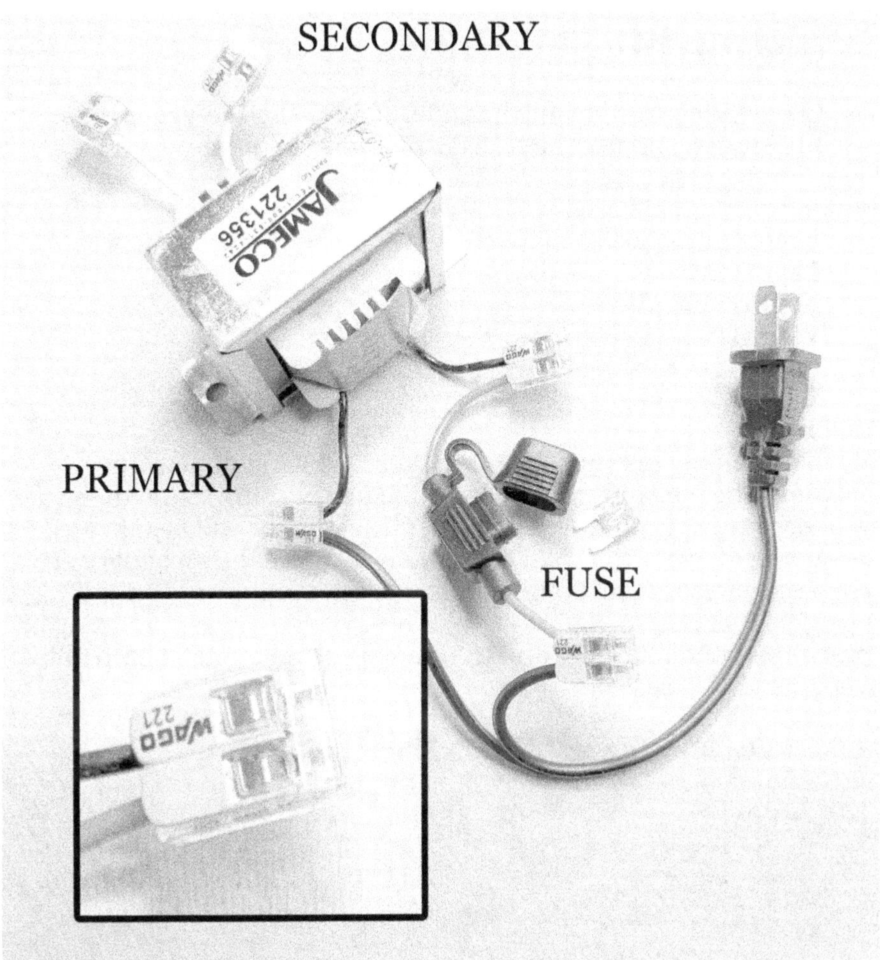

Testing
Make sure the secondary wires are not touching, and carefully plug
the lamp cord in for a second. Nothing should happen. If you get
sparks, blow a fuse, or your circuit breaker pops, make sure your plug
is wired to the primary, and the transformer is for 120V, and the
output wires are not touching and causing a short - that won't cause
sparks, but may pop the inline fuse and may smoke the transformer.
Once you have the lamp cord attached Land tested, the transformer
can be attached to a Version 1 or Version 2 etching machine.

Random Transformers
For a power transformer, the size and weight are related to the
voltage and amps. A transformer for 6V half amp is a lot smaller than
a 12V 2A, and a 24V 4A transformer is pretty chunky. With 6V and
half an amp, you can etch and mark, but 12V 2A is better.

12V 4A Etching Machine

The 12V 4A Etching Machine has one voltage. Use the Version 1 machine design and use the transformer instead of the adapter.

Parts
____ jameco.com part 221356 12V 4A, or Triad F-219X 12V 4A
____ Lamp Cord assembled with Fuse
____ Nichrome 80 Wire
____ WAGO 221-412 connectors
____ Plywood Mounting Board & Screws

Assembly
See the assembly instructions for making the Version 1 etching machine. The only difference here is the power source from the two secondary wires from the transformer; the resistor will be different depending on what you want. The two leads from the secondary are AC so the wires can be mounted just like the adapter.

Attaching the transformer and terminal block on a small board helps keep them in place.

Make a resistor for 12V with Nichrome 80 wire
```
 9"  28g   3R     4A  48W
12"  28g   4R     3A  36W
18"  28g   6R     2A  24W
24"  28g   8R  1.5A  18W
23"  30g  12R     1A  12W
```

Oh No! More Wires
If you have transformer with more than two wires on the primary side, it means they can be wired for other voltages. Get help with those. It's probably for 115V/220V.

Center Tap
Lots of transformers have more than two wires on the secondary. In the catalogs, you will see "CT" and it means "center tap", and many of them have 3 wires on the secondary that will output two different voltages.

A 12V CT makes 12V and 6V, and a 24V CT makes 24V and 12V.

The outer two wires are 24V, and an inner and outer are the 12V. The 24V machine in the next build is a little more involved, but can handle lots of different requirements.

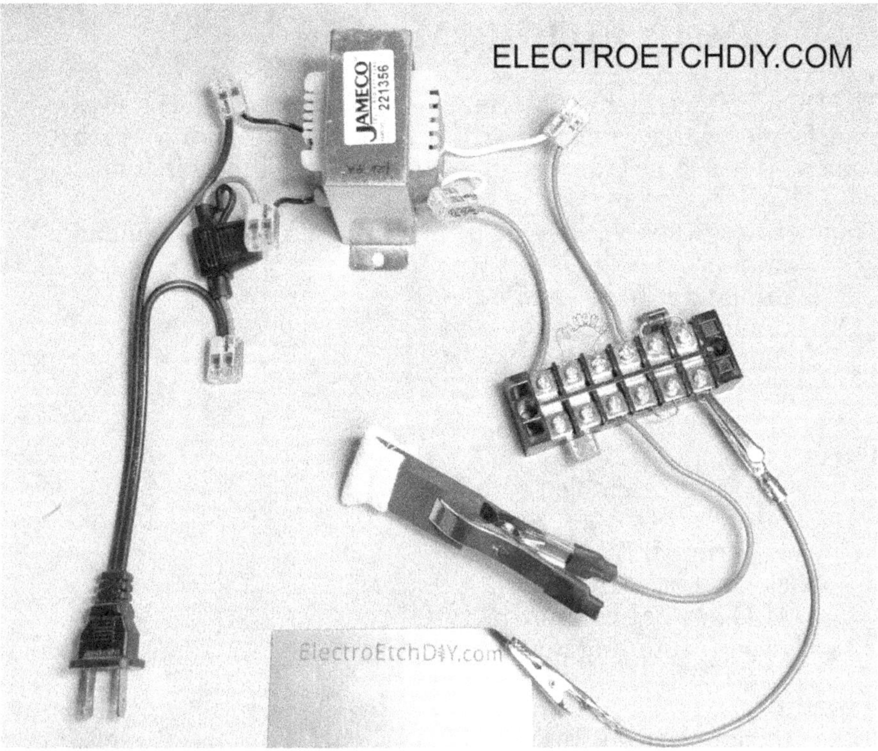

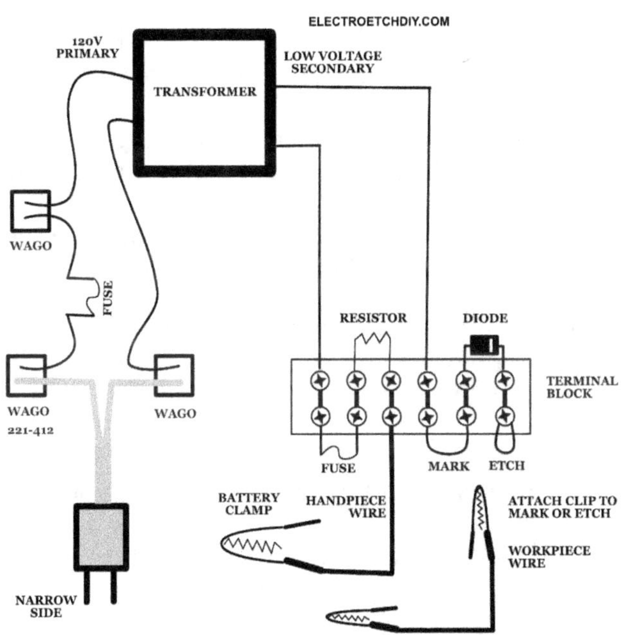
JAMECO
221356
ELECTROETCHDIY.COM
ElectroEtchDIY.com
ELECTROETCHDIY.COM
120V
PRIMARY
TRANSFORMER
LOW VOLTAGE
SECONDARY
WAGO
FUSE
RESISTOR
DIODE
WAGO
221-412
WAGO
TERMINAL
BLOCK
FUSE
MARK
ETCH
NARROW
SIDE
BATTERY
CLAMP
HANDPIECE
WIRE
ATTACH CLIP TO
MARK OR ETCH
WORKPIECE
WIRE

24V 12V 4A Etching Machine

The Dual Voltage Etching Machine has two voltages since it uses a transformer with a center tap. This design has a resistor for each voltage. It has to be mounted on a board to keep things in line.

Transformers: these are 2-wire primary (120V), 3 wire secondary.
____ Hammond 166N24 is 24V 4A CT
____ Hammond 166L24 is 24V 2A CT
____ Hammond 166N12 is 12V 4A CT
____ Hammond 166Q12 is 12V 6A CT
____ Others are available.

Parts
____ Lamp Cord assembled with Fuse
____ Solid Wire 18AWG
____ Two Terminal Blocks - 6 lug
____ Nichrome 80 Wire
____ WAGO 221-412 connectors
____ Plywood Mounting Board & Screws

Assembly
Attach the lamp cord with fuse to the primary. For this example, I'm using a 24V CT rated for 4A. It will provide 24V 4A, and 12V 4A.

See the drawing showing how the wires are attached to the terminal blocks. The outer wires are 24V, and an inner and outer wire are 12V.

Mount the transformer and two terminal blocks on a board with screws. I will call them Upper Terminal and Lower Terminal.

CONNECT wires (C1, C2, C3) are just solid 18g wires to bridge lugs. You can use stranded wire, but solid works better.

The Upper Terminal front has a bare wire lug for 24V and for 12V so you can move the alligator clip to select the voltage. It also has a wire resistor for the 24V and a wire resistor for the 12V.

The Lower Terminal Block has a bare wire ETCH lug and a bare wire MARK lug, and no resistor since they are on the upper block.

Make two resistors with Nichrome 80 wire
```
24V side: 18" 28g  6R 4A 96W *HOT*
12V side:  9" 28g  3R 4A 48W
```

See the chapter on resistors for lots of other options.

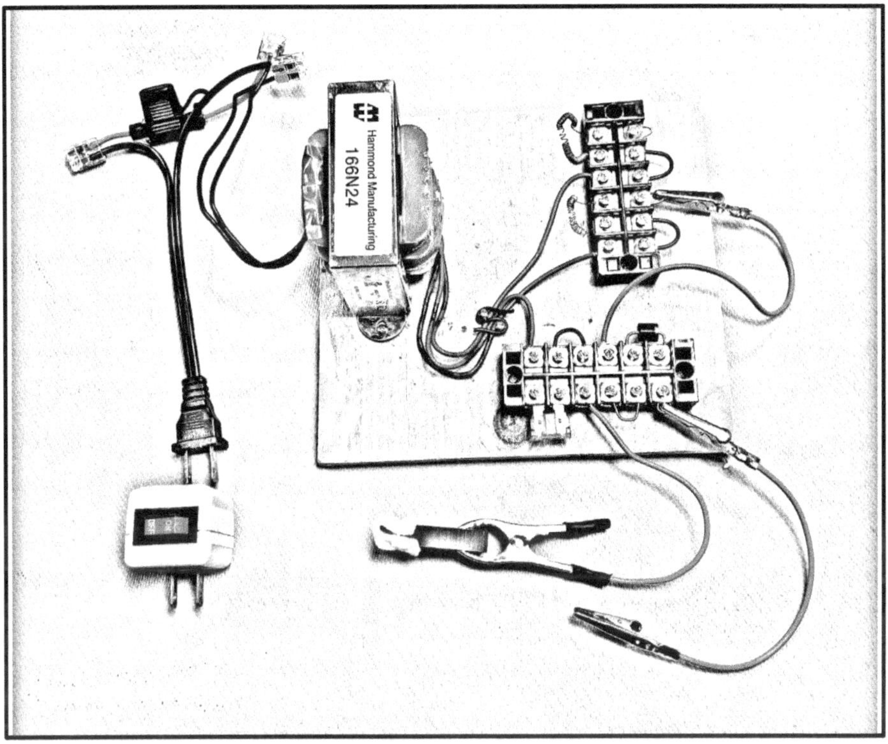

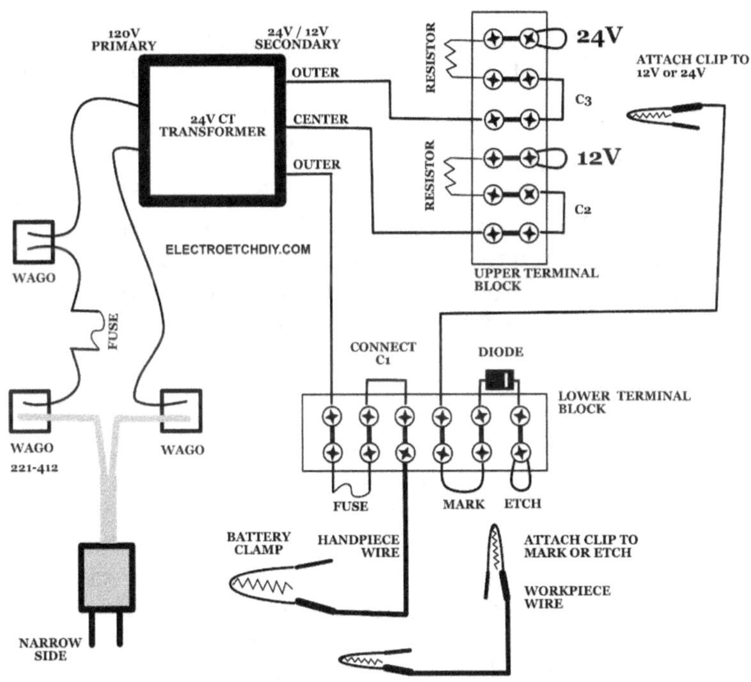
120V
PRIMARY
24V / 12V
SECONDARY
OUTER
CENTER
OUTER
24V CT
TRANSFORMER
ELECTROETCHDIY.COM
WAGO
WAGO
221-412
WAGO
FUSE
NARROW
SIDE
RESISTOR
RESISTOR
24V
C3
12V
C2
UPPER TERMINAL
BLOCK
ATTACH CLIP TO
12V or 24V
CONNECT
C1
DIODE
LOWER TERMINAL
BLOCK
FUSE
MARK
ETCH
BATTERY
CLAMP
HANDPIECE
WIRE
ATTACH CLIP TO
MARK OR ETCH
WORKPIECE
WIRE

Chapter 6 - Battery

Using a Battery for Electro Etching

A battery powered etching machine will etch stainless steel starting at about 3V. Most batteries will work, from a couple of 1.5V AAA, lead acid batteries, and tool batteries, like the one for your drill, up to 30V.

Voltage Measurement
To work with batteries, get an inexpensive multimeter to test the battery keep it from going too low.

Machine Version 2
Use machine Version 2 for batteries, and when you assemble it, connect the resistor and leads from the battery to the terminal block and get it all set up, THEN connect to the battery. Use 18g solid wire for the leads to the battery, so you can bend it into place and it stays put unless the battery holder already has leads.

Shorts
Be careful not to short a battery. A short is when the positive and negative touch, and it is not good. If they wiggle around, tape them down.

Use a Resistor and a Fuse
Use a resistor on the battery etching setups, just like for the adapters and transformers. The chapter on resistors has charts that make it easy to choose a wire gauge and length to make a good resistor, and there are suggestions for most of the batteries listed in this chapter. Making a resistor is easy - just winding the right length and gauge of wire on a rod to make a spring shape. A fuse can help if you make a wrong connection.

Battery Holders
A battery holder is the simplest way to make connections to batteries. Some have solder connections, leads, or tabs. If they are pre-wired, look for "series connections" to add the voltage together. Battery holders have a little plate or rivet end for the positive terminal, and a spring or a plate on the negative terminal. Try and find holders that allow you to remove the battery without hurting it. If it takes a screwdriver to pry out the battery, the wrapper can tear, and ruin it.

Shopping for battery holders, some listings show installed batteries, and some show a little extra room on the ends of the slots. They are easier to work with. Holders that have covers seem to be less tight. You can solder to the ends of carbon-zinc and alkaline batteries if you are quick about it; don't solder lithium or rechargeable batteries.

AAA, AA, C, D Battery

You can electro etch with two AAA, AA, C, or D batteries connected so they are 3V or more. Be patient with the etch, and the results are good. If you use carbon-zinc batteries, you can salvage the graphite rods.

Rechargeable NiMh are 1.2V so use three or four of them. Two can be frustrating - it is below 3V. Rechargeable lithium, lithium, carbon zinc, and alkaline batteries are each 1.5V, so two or more will work. If you are buying battery holders, get the four bay since the etch is quite a bit faster at 6V than 3V.

When you are working with 3V, the etch is not as fast, and smaller stencils work better since it is easier to make sure the entire stencil has had enough etch time.

```
VOLTS  AMPS  OHMS WATTS WIRE
  3V    2A   1.5R   6W   7"  26g Nichrome 80
  6V    3A     2R  18W  10"  26g Nichrome 80
```

9V Battery

The 9V radio battery etching works well for a little while.

```
VOLTS  AMPS  OHMS WATTS WIRE
  9V    2A   4.5R  18W  8.5"  30g Nichrome 80
 18V    2A     9R  36W   11"  32g Nichrome 80
```

14500 Battery

A neat little battery that is the same size as the AA is the 14500 and it is 3.6V. They should fit in the AA holders, and four of them are 15V. The rechargeable lithium ion are easy to get and not expensive, but get a charger for them.

```
VOLTS  AMPS  OHMS WATTS WIRE
 3.7V  2.5A  1.5R   8W   3"    30g Nichrome 80
 7.4V  2.5A    3R  18W  5.5"   30g Nichrome 80
  15V   3A     5R  45W  9.5"   30g Nichrome 80
```

18650 Battery

The 18650 battery is 3.6V and is very popular in DIY circles. It is used inside many battery packs and fancy flashlights. If you want to use them, get a compatible charger. You will also need a holder for them, and it's tricky. The holders for the 18650 will only handle the "flat top" which is 65mm long. Most flat top batteries don't have any protection built in for over-charge or over-discharge, so try not to let the voltage for each battery go below 2.5V. The "button top" version is about 67mm long and does not have protection built in, and the "button top protected" is about 70mm long and has built in protections. Only the basic flat top will fit the 18650 holders I can find. Using too small a holder will tear the insulating plastic off the battery when you pry it out. The holders for a 20700 battery should work on the protected button top 70mm battery since it's about the same length as a 20700 flat top. Limit your amps to the specs for the battery, or use 2A or 3A to be safe. Some of these batteries are 2A, some a lot more, and the better online stores will provide details.

```
VOLTS   AMPS   OHMS  WATTS  WIRE
 3.7V   2.5A   1.5R    8W   3"     30g Nichrome 80
 7.4V   2.5A     3R   18W   5.5"   30g Nichrome 80
  15V     3A     5R   45W   9.5"   30g Nichrome 80
```

Tool Battery

A tool battery can be your go-to for etching. They mostly have 18650 batteries inside (or newer sizes), and solve the complicated parts of using and charging them. There are lots of brands and voltages of tool battery and most should work. The neatest way to use a tool battery is an aftermarket adapter for big toy cars, also called powerwheels. They are a thing. Search on "dock adapter for Ryobi" (use your brand), and there is probably an adapter or it.

Use a multimeter to keep track of the voltage on your tool battery. To find the safe low voltage, run your battery down with your tool like normal, then measure the voltage on the battery. That should be the minimum you should let the battery go before you charge it again.

```
See the chapter on resistors to choose one for your voltage.
```

Lead Acid Battery

The lead acid batteries in deer feeders, boats, and cars all work for etching if used with a resistor. A good rule for these batteries is to use it if it has a regular other job. Borrow it for etching, then put it back so it can live a long happy life, but don't let it's voltage go below 12.4V. If you are getting a lead acid battery for electro etching, get a deep cycle battery and a charger for it.

Lithium Iron Phosphate Battery

The newer LiFePO4 with a BMS (battery management system) are pretty neat and 12V are easy get. They use a special charger, so get that at the same time. They can safely be used till they stop if they have a BMS, and can be used with a small inverter to run an AC etching machine.

```
VOLTS   AMPS   OHMS  WATTS  WIRE
  12V     2A     6R   24W   11"   30g Nichrome 80
  12V     3A     4R   36W   12"   28g Nichrome 80
  12V     4A     3R   48W    9"   28g Nichrome 80
```

Connections

If you need to make leads to the battery, use 18g solid wire for them so you can bend them into position and they tend to stay put. Don't short the leads or it can damage the battery.

Battery Life

If you get a rechargeable battery just for your etching machine, plan on charging it every few months. Just sitting for months can make the battery fail.

Battery Etching Machines

These use the Version 2 design, and a resistor allows them to work.

The 18V etching machine is using a Ryobi 18V battery and a dock.

The four D battery machine is using end to end battery holders that snap together.

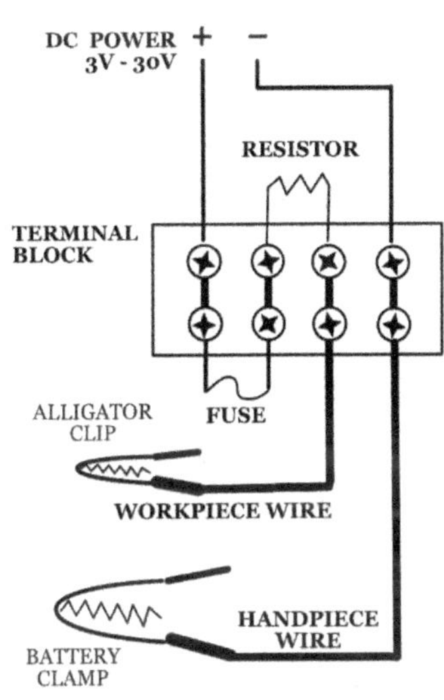

18V	**D Batteries**

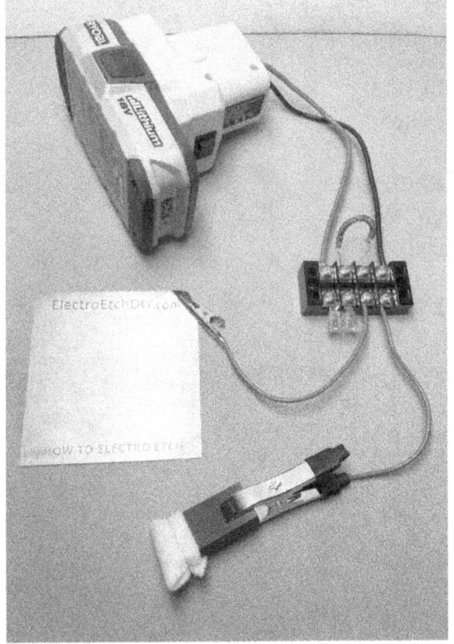

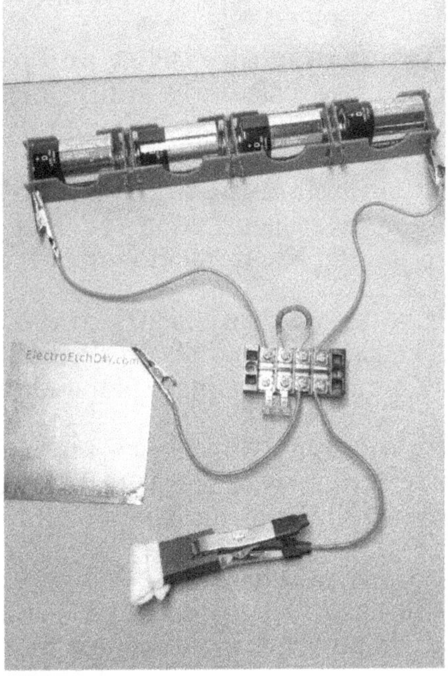

Chapter 7 - Using Other Power

Other Power Sources

A lot of different power sources are being used to electro etch, and here are a couple more. These are wired to the Version 2 etching machine.

Retrofit an Electro Etch Machine
If your electro etch machine does not have a way to control the amps, you can make it work better by adding a resistor. It is easy to set up by connecting it's outputs to a Version 2 etching machine, and you can connect your existing handpiece and workpiece wire to the terminal block.

Choosing a Resistor
If your machine is just one voltage, the resistor just has to work for the volts and amps available. If your machine has two voltages like 12V and 6V, or 24V and 12V, the resistor needs to work for both of them, and not melt. If it is dual voltage with a center tap transformer, then the amp rating is the same for both voltages.

If your machine is 12V and 6V at 1A
Use a 12R resistor: 1A at 12V, and .5A at 6V
14" of 32g Nichrome 80 for a 12R resistor

If your machine is 12V and 6V at 2A
Use a 6R resistor: 2A at 12V, and 1A at 6V
18" of 28g Nichrome 80 for a 6R resistor

If your machine is 12V and 6V at 3A
Use a 4R resistor: 3A at 12V, and 1.5A at 6V
12" of 28g Nichrome 80 for a 4R resistor

If your machine is 12V and 6V at 4A
Use a 3R resistor: 4A at 12V, and 2A at 6V
9" of 28g Nichrome 80 for a 3R resistor

If your machine is 24V and 12V at 4A
Use a 12R resistor: 2A at 24V, and 1A at 12V
18" of 28g Nichrome 80 for a 6R resistor

If you have an old 12V 10A battery charger
Use 24" of 22g Nichrome 80 for a 2R resistor for 6A at 12V
Use 18" of 28g Nichrome 80 for a 6R resistor for 2A at 12V
Use any 12V or higher resistor.

See the chapter on resistors to make a resistor for other voltage and
amp combos. Make sure your resistor works for both voltages, or you
may melt it. Change out the 5A fuse if you will be using more than it
can handle; 10A blade fuses are usually red. Use scrap wood under
the terminal block while testing so you don't burn the table.

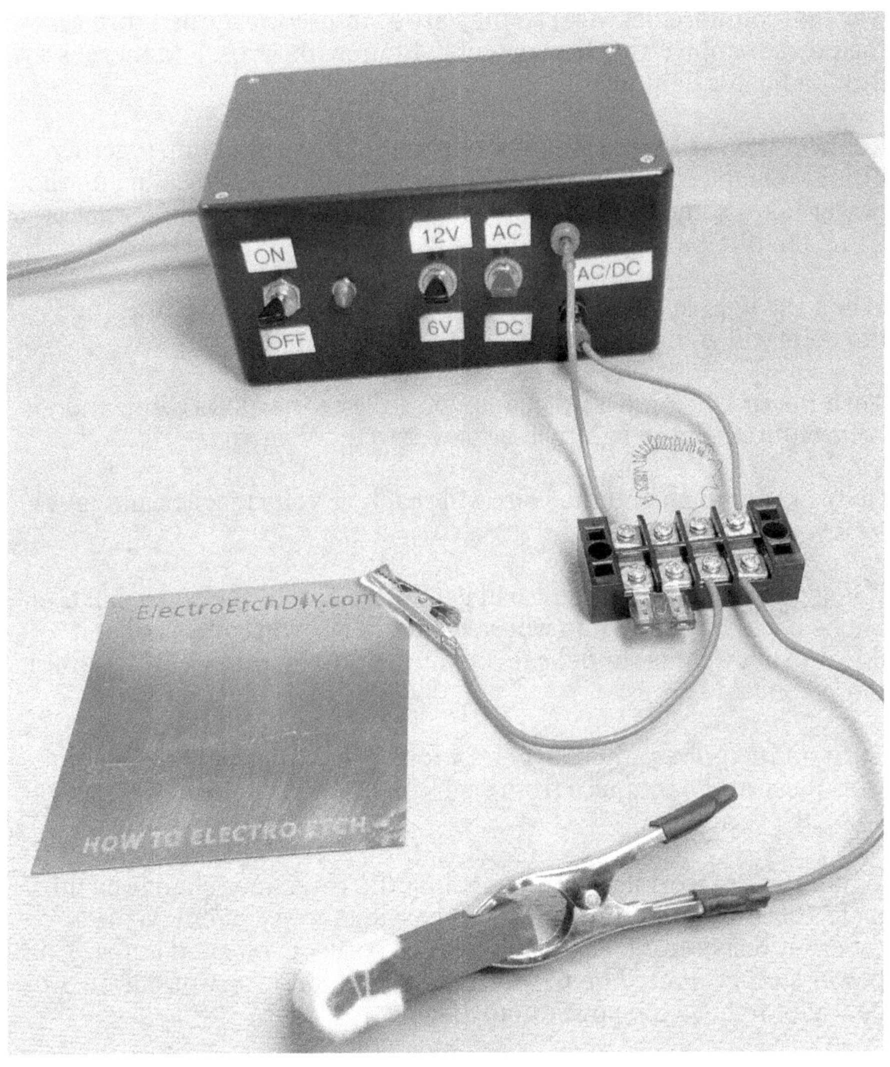

Using a Bench Power Supply

These machines are called bench power supplies or DC power supplies, and are used a lot in electronics workshops, and artists use them for vat style etching and plating. The one I have is branded as "Eventek" and is 30V 10A, model KPS3010D and is $60 to $70 on Amazon. If you can't find the exact one, get one that looks similar and is 30V and 10A and has an Amps knob and Volts knob.

To use a DC power supply for electro etching, use machine Version 2, and start with a 6R for 12V 2A resistor (11" of 30g Nichrome 80) on the Version 2 machine with scrap wood under the terminal block in case the resistor melts.

Turn the machine off, and dial the Voltage and Current knobs all the way off (counterclockwise) so they are at their lowest, then turn on the power supply; the display will light up with zeros, and there is a little indicator light next to the "V" or the "A".

Connect the workpiece alligator clip and handpiece clamp together. This closes the circuit so the power can be calibrated. Dialing up the power takes some fooling with since it's not exactly obvious what is going on, but it's easy.

When the light is next to the V, turn the **voltage** knob a little, and the volts will go up, and the indicator will hop to the amps A.

Turn the **amps** knob a little, and you will see the amps climb and the volts climb then the light will hop over to the V again.

Go back and forth and the volts will reach 12 volts reaches and 2A or so if you have a 6R resistor (12V / 6R = 2A).

If you go higher, the resistor will get hotter until it melts, so dial the knobs back to get down to where it should be. You can also dial it down to a few volts for delicate etching, or use a different resistor for more volts and amps.

Turn off the power, and leave the knobs where they are, detach the workpiece and handpiece from each other, and when you are ready to etch, just turn it on.

While you are working, you can watch the resistance change as the pad saturates and the stencil starts passing more current. With different resistors, you can etch with all sorts of volts and amps. This power supply is rated up to 30V at 10A, and for large work, it might be useful to have the power and voltage.

Connect to Version 2 Machine

Prepare two leads of 18g solid wire, stripping an inch off one end, and half an inch from the other. Make a hook from the longer bare ends and connect them to the power supply terminal and the other ends to the Version 2 etching machine, then install the 6R resistor. The positive wire connects to rear lug #1 just like a battery.

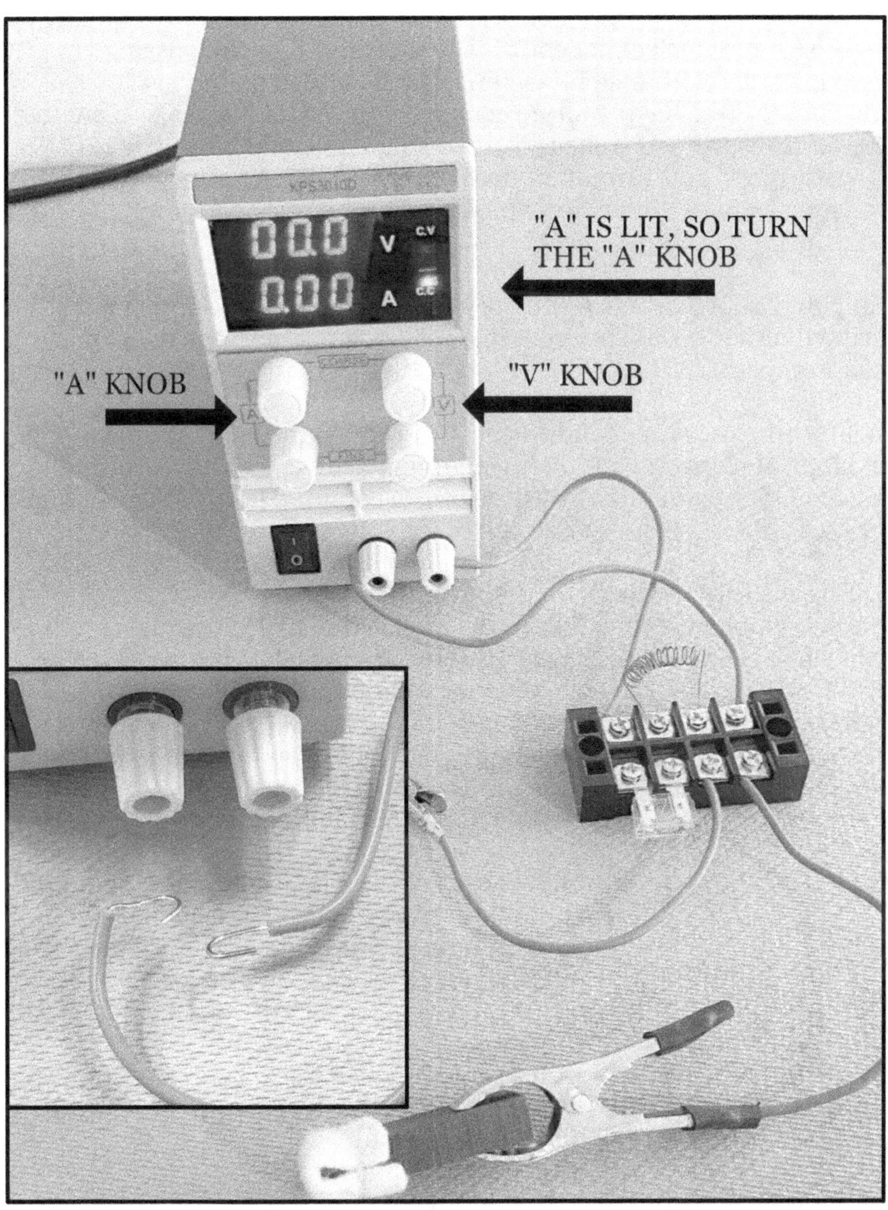

Chapter 8 - Resistors

How to Make Resistors

A resistor is a device that controls how many amps are passing
through your electro etch machine. Until I added one to my
machines, I was having all sorts of problems. Hot handpieces, melted
connections, ruined stencils, ruined adapters, and smoked
transformers, and I wouldn't dare try using a large battery. With a
resistor, I can use many low voltage power sources like adapters,
transformers, and batteries.

All power sources have a voltage and amp rating. For adapters, it's
printed on the case. The recommended etching machine uses an
adapter that is 12V 2A.

Controlling the amps (and watts) will control the heat. There are lots
of kinds of resistors, but for an etching machine, we can use a small
halogen light bulb if the machine uses a common bulb voltage like 6V,
12V, or 24V, or, use resistance wire for voltage from 3V to 30V.

Using a Light Bulb as a Resistor
A small halogen bulb will limit the power and is nice because it tells
you when electricity is flowing. Get the small bulbs with bi-pin leg,
and they will fit in the terminal block. Be sure the bulb voltage
matches the power source voltage (120V get mixed in the bin). If it's
another kind of bulb, then a fixture may be needed. When you attach
a bulb to the terminal block, gently tighten each leg so they line up so
it does not twist and shatter when it's tightened.

The bulb is technically a ballast, but is instantly a
resistor and limits the amps. Here are some
common options. If a bulb doesn't match up with
the volts and amps, use a wire resistor.

 6V 2A uses a 10W bulb
12V 1A uses a 10W bulb
12V 2A uses a 20W bulb
12V 3A uses a 35W bulb
24V 1A uses a 20W bulb

Resistance Wire
Nichrome 80 is special wire that has resistance and gets hot when electricity passes, so it's are popular in toasters; and it's easy to get rolls of wire online. Search for "Nichrome 80 28g". The wire is called "Nichrome 80" and the "80" makes a difference. Buy solid round wire (not a weave or flat). They sell by the roll ($7) and by the set. With a few different resistors, you can customize the power for any etching machine from just a few watts to many. Just loosen two screws, and switch out the resistor.

Resistor Charts
To make it easy, look in the charts for your voltage and the amps that are closest to the rated output of your power source.

The charts have voltage, amps, watts, wire type, gauge, and wire length in inches. Measure the length of wire, cut it, and wind it into a spring shape.

Gauge or AWG or g
The gauge or AWG is the thickness of the wire. Higher numbers are thinner and have more resistance, but handle fewer watts.

Voltage
The lists are grouped by voltage for some common adapters, batteries, and transformers.

Resistor Math
To keep this simple, I am using the W for Watts, A for Amps, R for Resistance, and V for Volts. If you study electronics, you'll learn the Ohm's Law letters.

Amps
Volts divided by Resistance gets you Amps:
12V / 6R = 2A

Watts
Volts times Amps gets you Watts:
12V * 2A = 24W

Resistance
Volts divided by Amps gets you Resistance: 12V / 2A = 6R

Power Rating
Power sources usually have some leeway for how much power they can handle. If you know you will be doing production work, choose a resistor so that the amps being pulled are not above it's rating. Some power sources are picky, and will stop working at any draw over the

rating, and some will let you get away with half again as much of a draw. Some have a fuse inside and will stop working forever, some stop for a few minutes. For batteries, assume 2A or 3A unless you know otherwise. Tool batteries are designed to handle lots of amps, but the heat will damage your stencils and make your handpiece hot.

For most etching, you will not pull the full amount of power because the stencil art, handpiece, pad wetness, and handpiece size all play into the power draw. The resistor prevents a big power draw.

The chart is from experiments, and the voltage and amps listed should not sag the wire or have glowing legs where they connect to the terminal block.

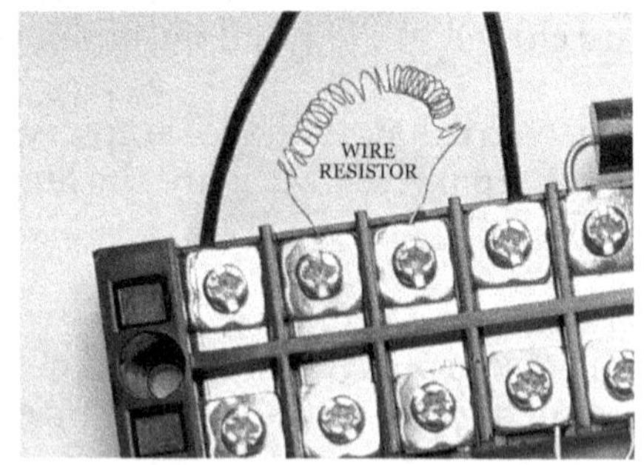

Most voltage/amp combos have more than one choice, and I try for the shortest wire, or the best use of a roll.

How to Make a Wire Resistor
Measure out the inches from the roll. You don't need to be exact, but when it's only a few inches, try and get close.

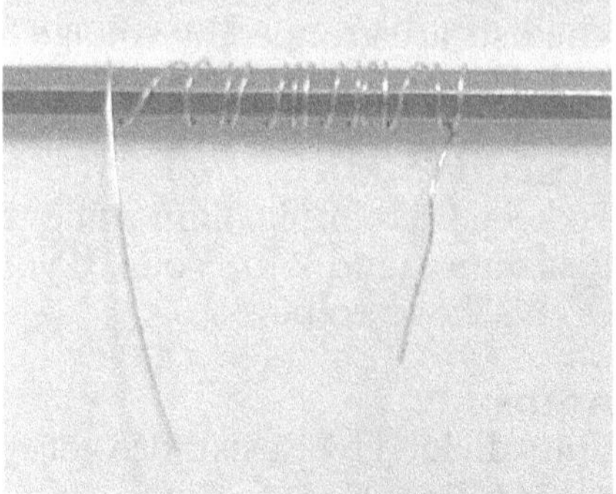

Wind the wire on a pencil or rod or hex wrench to make it look like a spring, and leave a leg on each end to attach to the terminal block. If any of the wire loops touch or overlap, spread them out a little.

The resistor coil should be in the air when it's mounted on the terminal block and should not be too close to the plastic terminal block or wires. If it is close to the block, unwind and extend the legs a little. They are easy to bend.

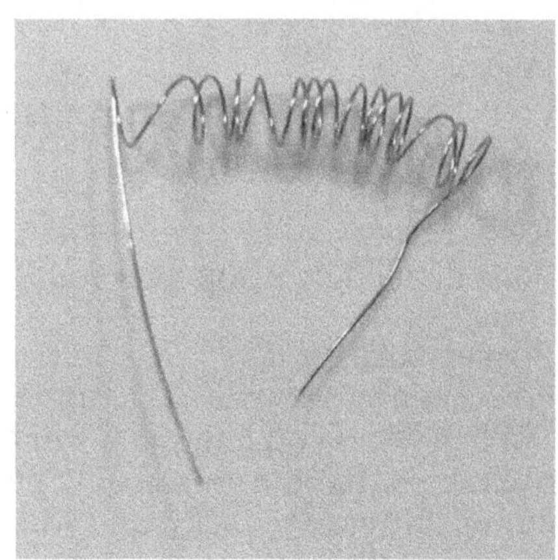

Burning in the Resistor

Each tail of the resistor will screw down into the terminal block with the spring standing up. Check that the wire is held in the lug, and move it to another spot under the clamp if needed (for really thin wire). Test it over a board so you don't damage your table if something is not right, and the wire melts.

Once it is screwed down, and before you power it up, attach the workpiece clip to the MARK lug and your handpiece clamp to the workpiece clamp (closes the circuit like the end of an etch), and power up and down quickly a few times. The wire will very lightly smoke the first time. Less than a match.

If you selected a resistor that can't handle your voltage, it will turn bright red and sag and melt, scorching whatever is under your terminal block.

Red spots will show when two coils are touching. Let it cool and move them apart. The wire is pretty tough, so just bend it. You want the heat to spread across all the coils. It may be red all the way across, but if the color is even, it's OK. The legs should not turn red except at the upper limits for the wire, and it should not happen unless you are burning in the resistor. If you are working on large stencils with a large handpiece, and the legs of the wire resistor are turning red, go to a thicker gauge wire from the charts.

Once the heat is even across the coils, turn the power on for a few seconds then turn it off. The resistor is durable and will last a long time. The wire will turn dark. While you are etching or marking, the wire will get hot but your power source will be OK because it's rated to handle the amps, or close enough. Towards the end of the etch or mark is when the maximum amps usually happen, and when the resistor will get hot. For most of your work, the wire will not turn red.

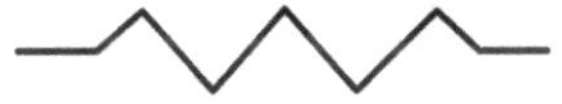

Resistor Ratings - Important

If a resistor works at a voltage, it will work for a lower voltage, but a higher voltage might melt it.

For example, a 6R resistor made from 18” of 28g Nichrome 80 will handle 24V, and any lower voltage like an 18V tool battery, or a 12V adapter. If you use it on 30V it may melt.

Resistor Lists

These resistors cover a wide range of voltages, and there are lots of ways to reach the same resistance by changing the length and gauge.

Resistors for 3V

```
AMPS   OHMS  WATTS  WIRE
  1A    1R    3W     5" 26g Nichrome 80
  2A  1.5R    6W     7" 26g Nichrome 80
  4A  .75R   12W     6" 24g Nichrome 80
```

Resistors for 6V (or less)

```
AMPS   OHMS  WATTS  WIRE
 .5A   12R    3W    14" 32g Nichrome 80
  1A    6R    6W    11" 30g Nichrome 80
  2A    3R   12W     9" 28g Nichrome 80
  3A    2R   18W    10" 26g Nichrome 80
  4A  1.5R   24W     7" 26g Nichrome 80
  6A    1R   36W     5" 26g Nichrome 80
```

Resistors for 9V (or less)

```
AMPS   OHMS  WATTS  WIRE
  1A    9R    9W    17" 30g Nichrome 80
  2A  4.5R   18W   8.5" 30g Nichrome 80
  3A    3R   27W     9" 28g Nichrome 80
  4A  2.3R   36W     7" 28g Nichrome 80
  6A  1.5R   54W     7" 26g Nichrome 80
```

Resistors for 12V (or less)

```
AMPS   OHMS  WATTS  WIRE
  1A   12R   12W    14" 32g Nichrome 80
1.5A    8R   18W    10" 32g Nichrome 80
  2A    6R   24W    11" 30g Nichrome 80
2.5A    5R   30W    15" 28g Nichrome 80
  3A    4R   36W    12" 28g Nichrome 80
3.5A  3.4R   42W    10" 28g Nichrome 80
  4A    3R   48W     9" 28g Nichrome 80
  6A    2R   72W    10" 26g Nichrome 80
  8A  1.5R   96W    12" 24g Nichrome 80
 10A  1.2R  120W    15" 22g Nichrome 80
```

Resistors for 14V (or less)

```
AMPS   OHMS  WATTS  WIRE
  1A   14R   14W    17" 32g Nichrome 80
  2A    7R   28W     9" 32g Nichrome 80
  3A  4.7R   42W     9" 30g Nichrome 80
  4A  3.5R   56W    11" 28g Nichrome 80
  6A  2.3R   84W    11" 26g Nichrome 80
  8A  1.8R  112W    14" 24g Nichrome 80
 10A  1.4R  140W    17" 22g Nichrome 80
```

Resistors for 18V (or less)

```
AMPS   OHMS  WATTS  WIRE
  1A   18R   18W    21" 32g Nichrome 80
1.5A   12R   27W    14" 32g Nichrome 80
  2A    9R   36W    11" 32g Nichrome 80
  3A    6R   54W    11" 30g Nichrome 80
  4A  4.5R   72W    14" 28g Nichrome 80
  6A    3R  108W    14" 26g Nichrome 80
  8A  2.3R  144W    17" 24g Nichrome 80
 10A  1.8R  180W    22" 22g Nichrome 80
```

Resistors for 20V (or less)

```
AMPS   OHMS  WATTS  WIRE
  1A   20R    20W   24" 32g Nichrome 80
1.5A   13R    30W   16" 32g Nichrome 80
  2A   10R    40W   12" 32g Nichrome 80
2.5A    8R    50W   15" 30g Nichrome 80
  3A  6.5R    60W   12" 30g Nichrome 80
  4A    5R    80W   15" 28g Nichrome 80
  6A  3.3R   120W   16" 26g Nichrome 80
  8A  2.5R   160W   19" 24g Nichrome 80
```

Resistors for 24V (or less)

```
AMPS   OHMS  WATTS  WIRE
  1A   24R    24W   28" 32g Nichrome 80
1.5A   16R    36W   19" 32g Nichrome 80
  2A   12R    48W   14" 32g Nichrome 80
2.5A  9.5R    60W   18" 30g Nichrome 80
  3A    8R    72W   15" 30g Nichrome 80
  4A    6R    96W   18" 28g Nichrome 80
  6A    4R   144W   19" 26g Nichrome 80
```

Resistors for 30V (or less)

```
AMPS   OHMS  WATTS  WIRE
  1A   30R    30W   35" 32g Nichrome 80
  2A   15R    60W   18" 32g Nichrome 80
  3A   10R    90W   19" 30g Nichrome 80
  4A  7.5R   120W   23" 28g Nichrome 80
```

Other Voltages

If your power source has a voltage that is not on the list below, just choose a resistor from any higher voltage, and calculate the amps it will draw.

Divide the voltage by the resistance R, and get the amps it will try to draw.

Volts / Resistance = Amps

Volts * Amps = Watts

Example: 16V 2A adapter

The next higher resistors are for 18V
16V / 9R = 1.8A so about right
16V / 6R = 2.7A is more than 2A
16V / 4.5R = 3.6A is too much

Example: 24V 2A CT transformer

The resistor has to work for both 24V and 12V, so choose from the 24V list

The 12R resistor is 24V / 12R = 2A and 12V / 12R = 1A so it will work.

Chapter 9 - Stencils

How to Make Stencils

A stencil for electro etching controls where electricity and electrolyte can pass. A good stencil will protect the undecorated surface, and after an etch or mark, there should not be pits, shading, smudging, or surface changes that are not expected. There may be a halo around the edges of the cut after an etch. A good stencil should not require any polishing except to remove a halo sometimes. A mark should not need any polishing, just a good wipe-down with a wet paper towel since it does not create a halo.

If you watch videos on electro etch, if the surface starts out normal then has to be cleaned up outside of where the etch or mark is, the stencil or resist is not blocking all the electricity. In some cases the stencil was almost good enough and the blemishes are just shallow shadows that will buff or sand out. For a mark, buffing out the rest of the blemish might take the artwork with it. A stencil that can be used for an etch that will be sanded afterwards doesn't work for a mark.

The stencil is by far the hardest part of electro etching, but thermal stencils are pretty easy. There are lots of stencil methods, but I will only focus on ones I have spent time with.

If you are using a computer, my favorite graphics program is called Affinity Photo, for both Mac/PC. The website is serif.com or the app stores. It is a one time cost, and there are lots of great tutorials online.

Stencil Art
Art for electro etching will take some experimenting to get right as it gets more detailed. Monograms and silhouettes are usually easy, but if your art has shading, the hatching or dots have to be far enough apart to be distinct in the stencil for the size you plan on using it. Screen and thermal stencils can handle more detail than vinyl stencils. To make artwork so that it can be electro etched it may need to be modified and converted to a sketch or line drawing. Search on "convert photo to sketch" to find tools to maybe help. Changing the dots per inch, or DPI to 300 can solve jagged edge problems.

Text and Fonts

Some fonts have lots of hanging bits, and are call "serif fonts", and some don't, and are called "sans serif fonts". Times New Roman is a serif font; this book font is Georgia, and it is serif. Arial is sans serif. When the text is larger in a stencil, either one is fine, but as text gets small, the hanging bits can get lost and the characters might start to look funny. Smaller text does better without the serif bits. There is also something called a "stencil font" that is designed so the parts are held together when it's cut; vinyl stencils work well with them.

If you are etching small text, it helps to spread the letters apart. It makes the stencil better, and the etch or mark easier to read. Your graphics program can do that. Look for the option called tracking.

<table>
<tr><td>Electro Etching</td><td>normal spacing</td></tr>
<tr><td>Electro Etching</td><td>spaced apart works better</td></tr>
<tr><td>ETCH</td><td>sans serif font</td></tr>
<tr><td>ETCH</td><td>serif fonts have bits hanging off</td></tr>
<tr><td>Open</td><td>stencil font</td></tr>
</table>

Halftone

If you look at a magazine or newspaper under a magnifier you will see images are made up of dots. That's called halftone. To make a stencil with halftone, the dots have to be far enough apart to be distinct.

Test Print On Paper

When you print out your artwork on paper at the size you plan to use as a stencil, check it over carefully to make sure it looks good. If it's jagged, increase the dots per inch to 300 DPI if possible.

Art and Amps

The amount of stencil open space in the art and the handpiece size, will affect how much power passes. A large stencil with lots of open area will pull more power than stencils with fine lines. A small handpiece will pull less power than a larger handpiece. The resistor keeps things from over heating.

Types of Stencils

Resists

A resist is the oldest (ancient) form of controlling where an etch occurs. Before electro etching, it was used for acids, and still is. It works well for acid. For electricity, I have tested dozens of coatings including waxes, floor polish, paint, inks, primers, paints ... and I have not found one I like. Either the coating shreds and drags the edges along and does not scribe cleanly, or it does not resist the electricity, and makes pits or marks outside the design. It has to resist the electrolyte and electricity and a little heat, plus the handpiece pad movement.

Impact Stencils

An older type of stencil material that can be scribed with a ballpoint pen is called an impact stencil. It is used with typewriters or by hand. Martronics sells a packet of 100 of them for not a lot. Use a ball point pen on it and press hard. If you put a flat steel plate under it, the results are pretty good. They work well for fast simple sorts of things, like inspections, or identification marks like initials.

Vinyl Stencils

The cutting machines by Cricut and Silhouette are very popular, and make a nice stencil if the art isn't too detailed or if you are really talented. I include painters tape stencils in this group. See the chapter on them.

Screen Stencils

The most common electro etch stencil is a screen stencil. It is made of a fine screen with a special coating. Screen stencils can make nice etches because they hold up to electricity and some heat. They need to be exposed, developed, and washed out. Emulsion sheets have to be purchased. The chapter on screen stencils has how to make them, including all about UV exposure units and making your own developer solution.

Thermal Stencils

Thermal stencils are the easiest. They can be printed with a computer or made with a special copier. After you get set up, they are fast, cheap, and easy to make. See the chapters on making them.

Stencil Spacing

Laying out the art on a stencil can make a big difference. Leave some space around the art so that your handpiece pad does not go beyond the stencil that is protecting your metal.

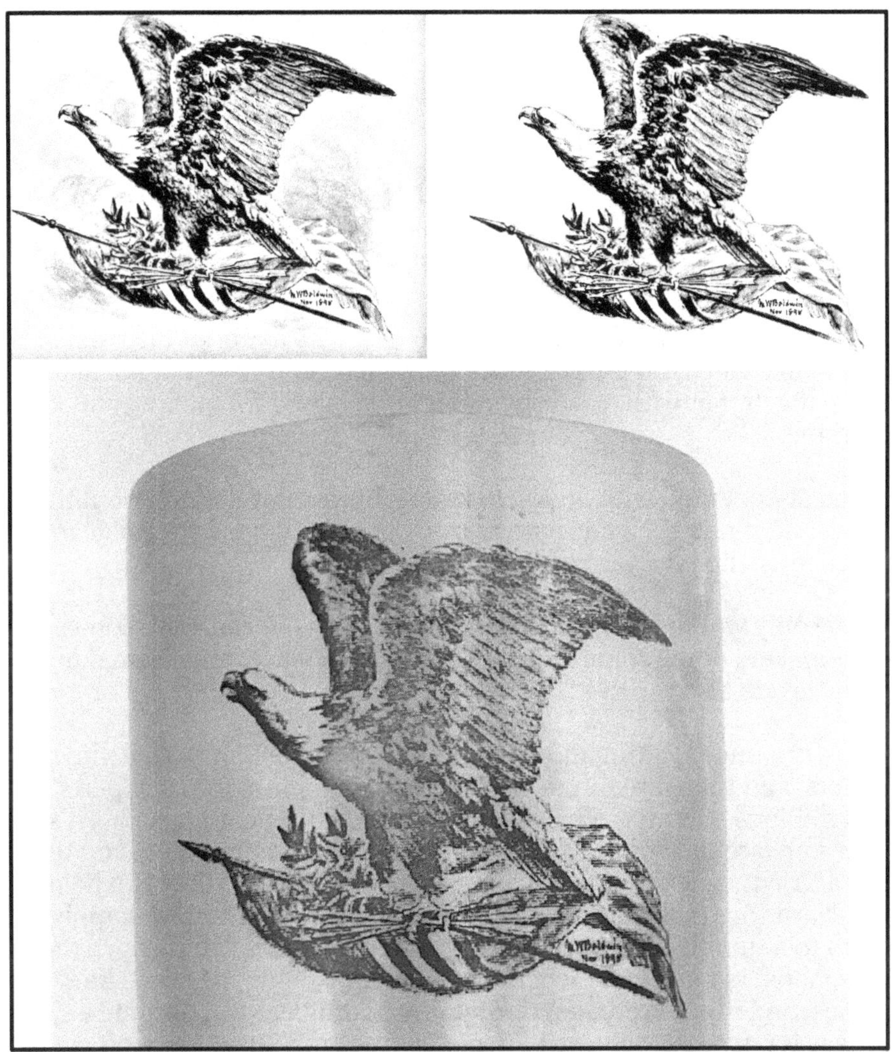

Old Etching on a Tumbler

A thermal stencil can handle a lot of fine detail, and sometimes it helps to remove parts that don't work well for an etch. Above is art from the late 1800's on a tumbler. Convert the art to black and white if needed, and then clean it up. The good thing is that with thermal, and thrift store steel, it's almost free to test it and see if it works. For new artwork, look into Etsy and search for vector or svg files.

There are lots of very talented artists selling files that will etch and mark with thermal, and some art works with vinyl or screen stencils.

Chapter 10 - Vinyl Stencils

How to Make Vinyl Stencils

Vinyl stencils work well for electro etching. The material is a plastic sort of like electrical tape. It blocks electricity and does not fall apart when it gets wet with electrolyte so it is very good for etching and marking.

If you are talented with an Xacto knife, you can cut designs from the vinyl, and if not, the vinyl cutters by Cricut and Silhouette make an excellent stencil for a lot of art.

I have only worked with vinyl a little bit so far, but there are some knifemakers doing some amazing things with vinyl stencils, making many layers of art with it.

There is a huge crafting industry around computer controlled vinyl cutters, and there are hundreds of videos on them done by experts, and millions of crafts folk using them. Each cutter company has it's own software, machines, and YouTube stars. If you have a friend that has a Cricut or Silhouette machine, or another brand, they can help you learn the tricks, make stencils for you, and even help you apply them to a tumbler or knife before you etch or mark. I think once the scrapbookers and glass etchers start electro etching there will be some wonderful art created on stainless. Tumblers will become a canvas for art that will last a long long time, and never peels off.

Vinyl material comes in a few brands and lots of versions, including permanent, light adhesive, no adhesive, all different colors; and a see-through vinyl called "stencil vinyl", that is not quite as sticky and can position more easily. Most vinyl should work, but maybe not glitter or metallic or exotic materials. Each one takes some learning to use with your cutter, so practice first.

The machines are also called die-cut machines, and the small ones for stencils are less than $200. Before you buy one, watch a few videos to see what the software looks like and how hard it is to learn. The two biggies, Cricut and Silhouette don't require CAD expertise to use them. Some machines have a steep learning curve for the software.

Stencil Art for Vinyl

Making vinyl stencils is not hard if the art is not complicated with lots of tiny details. The more tiny parts, the more skill it takes to cut it and remove the inside parts, also called weeding. It takes practice to get the settings right for the cutting head, and get your art files ready for the vinyl. Watch some videos on it; there are some great teachers who will introduce all of it to you.

Detailed stencils take skill to make and to use, and lucky for us there are lots of people making custom vinyl. Some kinds of art is really good for vinyl and some is more difficult. The more detail, the more involved it is to cut and to apply. For an example of difficult vinyl art, you want to etch or mark "MADE BY MOE" on a knife in a 14pt Arial font and all caps - a perfectly reasonable size for a thermal or screen stencil.

Here it is in 14pt Arial:　　**MADE BY MOE**

For a vinyl stencil, the letters are cut from the plastic, and must be plucked (weeded) leaving open spaces where the etch is. For "M" the letter would be removed in one piece, leaving a stencil opening for "M". Tweezers can just lift the letter out.

Some are easy like the "E" "Y" "M" ... but ... "A", "D", "B", and "O" have insides that have to stay in place or the letter will be filled in with an etch. The inside parts on a couple of those letters are tiny, and the cut has to be perfect since it is cutting both sides of the lines of the letter, and when it's weeded it's a precision process. The inside parts that stick to the steel at the top of the A, inside the D and O, and the even smaller parts inside the B have to be perfect, or it won't look right. Larger art works better. Stencil fonts connect the inside part to the background so it can be removed more easily. Search on "stencil fonts". As the text gets larger, holding the inside parts in place gets easier.

Transfer Vinyl

There is a special material called "transfer vinyl" that is sticky, and used to move the cut vinyl from it's sheet to the surface it is being applied to. Watch some videos on how this is done. After you cut your artwork, lay a piece of transfer vinyl over it and smooth it out, then lift the art from the backing paper. The vinyl will stick to the transfer vinyl. As the art is being lifted, some artists separate the parts so just the vinyl you want to "transfer" is on the upper layer, and some artists keep all of it on the upper layer. The stencil (stuck to the transfer vinyl) is then placed on the tumbler or knife, and smoothed out, then the transfer vinyl is carefully lifted, leaving the cut vinyl on the tumbler. During the lift, it can be weeded, or it can be weeded afterwards. For tiny parts like the inside of a letter, it has to stay on the steel and in the right place.

It takes practice, but applying vinyl to craft projects is the same as applying it to a steel tumbler, so friends that use it for mugs and picture frames and scrapbooking can help you apply it. After your etch or mark, the vinyl will probably only be good for one use.

Custom Vinyl

You can order custom vinyl stencils, and the seller may be able to help you with the art. Ask about how hard it will be to apply; to an experienced vinyl crafter, it may be easy, but ask if beginners can apply it, and get some extras.

Screen Mask

Another way to use vinyl is as a mask for making screen stencils. Dark vinyl does not pass light, and the artwork can be transferred to a clear sheet of film like overhead projector film, or a transparency. Once it is on the clear film, it can be used over and over as a mask to block UV while making screens. When you are exposing, put the vinyl face down on the screen film. Fewer light rays will sneak in. That will make sense if you make your own screen stencils.

Vinyl Cutters

I have the Cricut Joy machine since it is small, and makes stencils big enough for tumblers. It needs a computer and its software to send files to the cutter but it is easy to learn for the basic stuff I've done with it. Watch some videos on it since it's not exactly obvious what the steps are. Each material has special settings, and for detailed work, it can take some experimenting.

Sticky Stencil

One of the things vinyl does really well is stick to metal. One of the ways to mess up your etch or mark is moving the stencil even a tiny little bit. For a lot of art, a vinyl stencil may be the perfect tool for doing an etch. You can work the entire surface of the art, and you can see every detail.

Deeper Etching

Vinyl is very good for deeper etching since the adhesive keeps the edges of the cuts clean, and the plastic (and some tapes) resist electricity and normal heat. You can check your etching progress by wiping gently with a wet paper towel. Tumblers do better with a mark than they do with an etch. There is more contrast.

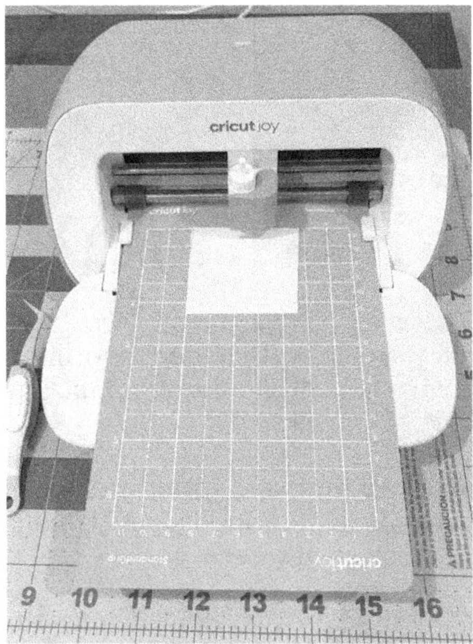

A Cricut Joy vinyl cutter will make a good stencil. Art that works best does not have tiny details, or thin lines, and it takes some practice to learn to use it.

The monogram shown here is easy to make. The mark is kind of splotchy because I was testing an electrolyte, and it's not as even as it should be.

I include it so you can see what to watch for. It's a little darker than saltwater and vinegar, but not as even.

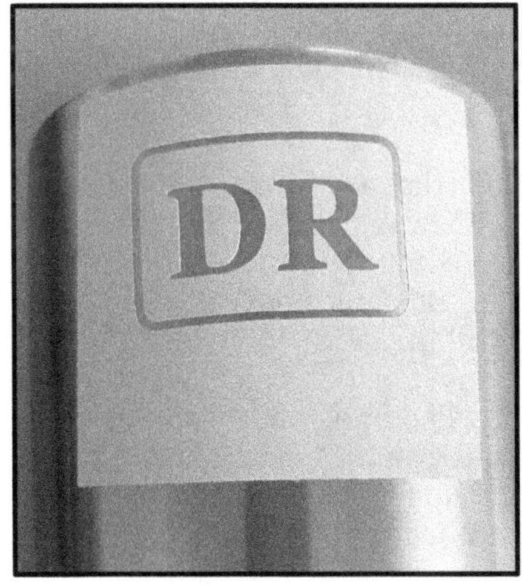
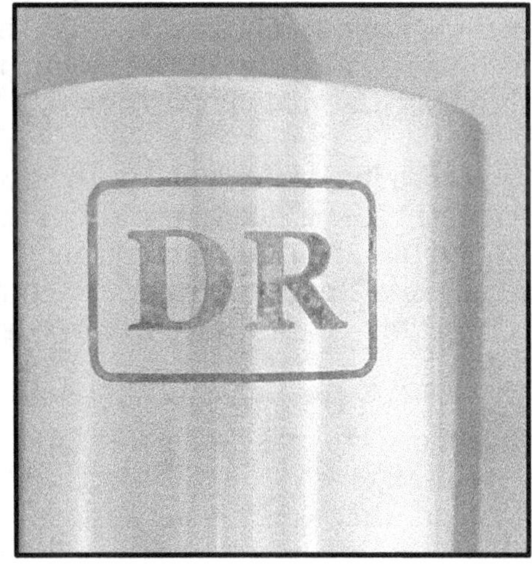

Chapter 11 - Thermal Stencils

How To Make Thermal Stencils

A thermal stencil uses a special paper with a coating that is heat sensitive and can be "printed" with a thermal printer. Instead of the black marks on thermal paper (like shipping labels and receipts), it opens up the coating, making a stencil.

Thermal stencils are great for marking and etching, but are not as durable as vinyl or screen film, so for deeper etching, screen or vinyl stencils are better, but thermal stencils make a nice etch or mark.

If you see extra tiny dots where they don't belong, the stencil is breaking down. Use less power and maybe less voltage if you have a higher voltage machine. For important work, I use a thermal stencil once. Don't rub it as you etch or mark, just use your handpiece up and down down or with a rolling motion.

Printing thermal stencils requires a special printer. There are a few options - a label printer, the 4x6 postage printer, the sales rep printer, and the tattoo printer. The label printer requires a special cartridge, and the others use a wider material that comes in rolls.

Thermal Stencils with a Label Maker
There are several videos on using the label-maker stencils for etching and marking, with mixed results. The results are mixed because many etching machines produce too much power. The heat will break through a thermal print.

There is a line of label makers by Brother that are called "P-Touch" and print sticky labels, and also take a stencil cartridge. The model PT-P700 is about $80 and prints from a computer, and handles the largest size stencil cartridge. A few other machines have a USB connection; check what size cartridge will fit.

The Brother USA website has all the detailed information and drivers (downloads to make a device work). Your graphics program can print to it just like any other printer, but with smaller paper settings. Once you find what works, you can save it as a printer paper size.

Stencil Cartridges

To buy the cartridges, look for the "ste-161 stencil" or the other sizes. STE-141 for 18mm, STE-151 for 24mm, and STE-161 for 36mm. It will say "Stencil Tape" on the picture of the cartridge. Look on eBay and Amazon. They are off brands and something like $16.

These printers create a very nice stencil that works for both etching and marking. They print so the glossy side is down, so you don't have to reverse things. Resize your art to 300 DPI if you can.

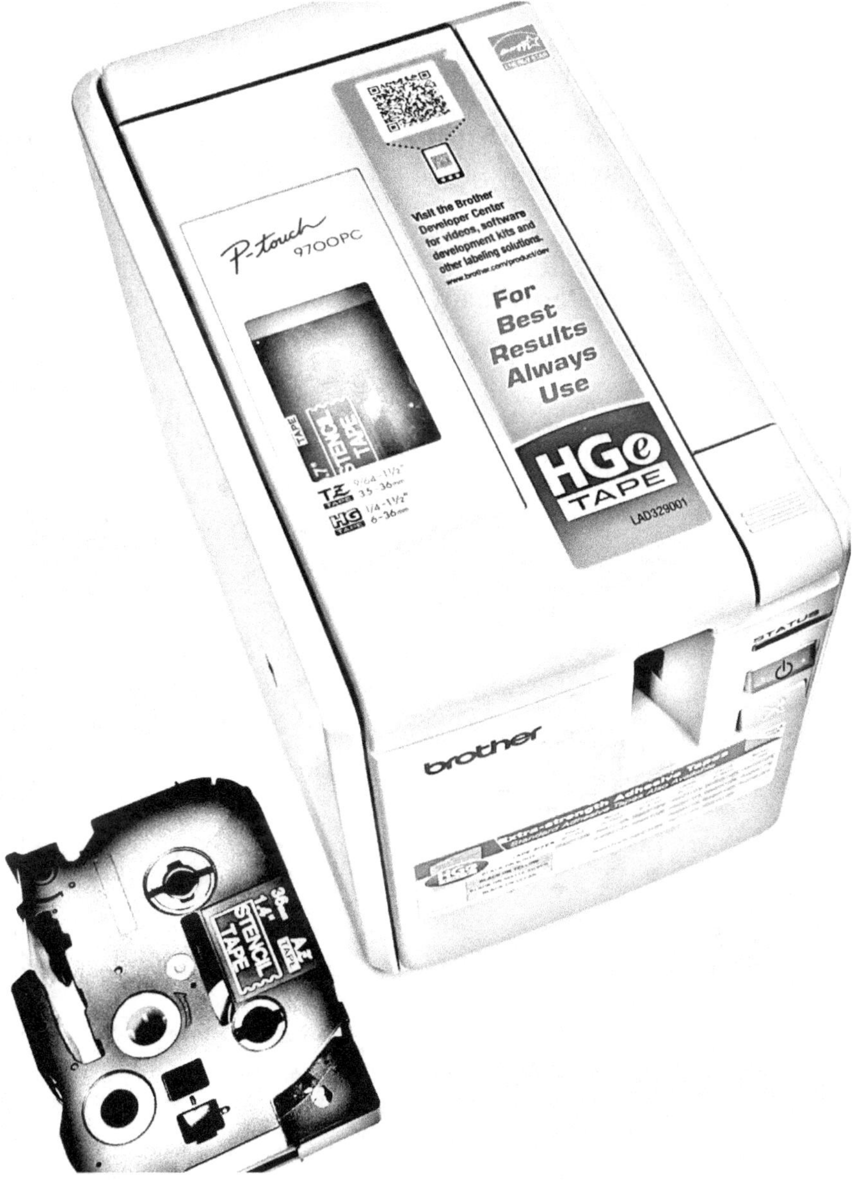

Buying Thermal Stencil Paper
Wide rolls of stencil material are available cheap. It is the same looking material as in the little printer cartridge. There is an office machine called a "duplicator". The stencil material has a very thin tangle of fibers that is coated with a very thin layer of glossy stuff. The rolls of material are called "master rolls", and are mostly letter size. The machine creates a stencil and presses ink through it to print many many copies. At some point the naming convention for a master roll may change, but if you understand what to look for, you'll find it.

The duplicators are made by Riso, Gestetner, Savin, Duplo, AB Dick, Ricoh, Nashuatec, and some others. The names are useful when searching eBay for the rolls, and there are many choices on eBay and Amazon. It doesn't matter what size or brand or product number you get, or new or old, just make sure it is not the ink, and not expensive. Search "duplicator master roll" or "Riso master roll" or "Ricoh master" or "Duplo master". It is white filmy stuff on a roll. You may find that some rolls print better with a little higher or lower temperature since there are many models of duplicator and they have slight differences.

A couple of rolls of thermal master paper costs from $10 to $55 on eBay; sort on low price to find it. A box with two rolls is enough to share with friends, and make many hundreds of tumbler stencils.

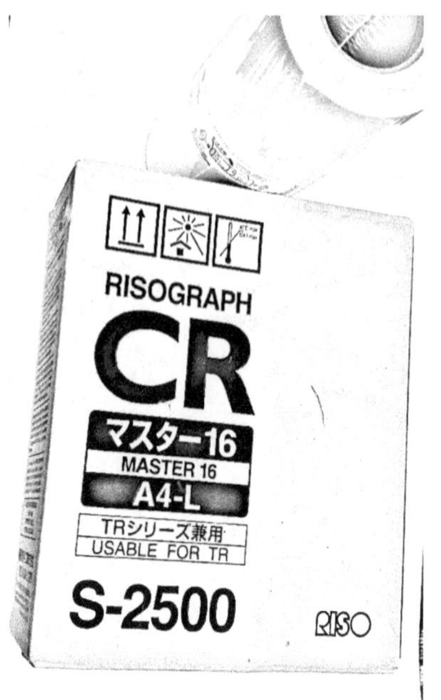

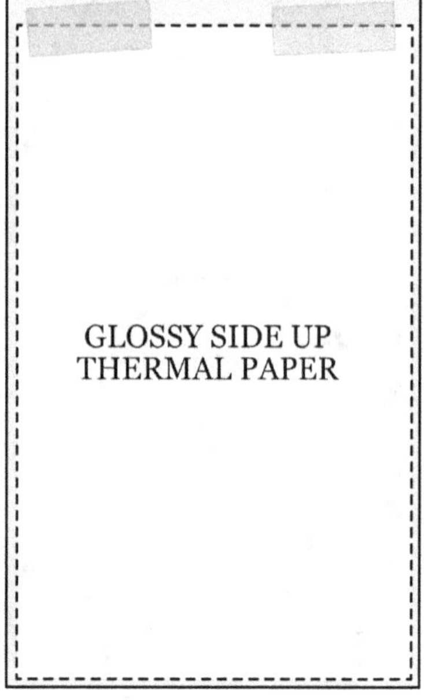

Thermal Stencils With Postage Printer

A 4x6 postage printer can use thermal stencil material cut from rolls. The printer connects to your computer, and there are lots on Amazon and eBay and some websites that specialize in refurbished postage printers.

To use a postage printer, attach a 4x6 piece of thermal material glossy side up to white paper the same size, and tape the leading edge to the white paper so it will feed. Use clear tape. The backing paper is for the sensors that look for paper.

Once you have a piece of stencil paper taped to a piece of plain paper, remove the roll of labels, and place the leading taped edge of the the stencil & paper right at the cut bar, glossy side up. The print head is at the front on the upper half, and will have "hot" markings.

When you close the printer, you should be able to print to it. If it does a sheet feed, see if there is an option to turn it off, or, cut a longer piece of white paper, and a longer stencil paper. I have an old refurbished Zebra printer I use for postage, and made my early thermal stencils with it. See the previous page for a drawing of how to mount the thermal paper. The sales rep printer uses the same method.

Adjusting the Label Printer

If the art is ragged (the edges not crisp), adjust the darkness in your print settings so it is less dark. You should see no ragged or pulled edges in the stencil. You can set the darkness in advance to less than the default. The settings will be different for each printer, but they should be easy to find in the print dialog window that comes up when you select the printer. Reverse the image in your graphics program before you print it so the glossy side will be down while you mark and etch.

Buying a 4x6 Printer

Some of these printers are locked to certain software or equipment. There are companies that sell refurbished ones, and stand by them. Get a USB connection cable and power supply from them, and ask if it will work with your computer and ask if any program can print to it, or if it is locked down to special software. The price should be less than $150.

Unless you need a postage printer and only do an occasional etching, the PocketJet or tattoo printer is better.

Thermal Stencils with a Mobile Printer

The PocketJet series of thermal printers by Brother are used as a mobile printer. It connects to your computer, uses thermal paper, and will also print a thermal stencil. It is letter size, but it's easy to use smaller strips of thermal stencil. This is probably the best option for regular stencil making if you use a computer.

Buying a Sales Rep Printer

Used thermal printers are available on eBay. They don't have ink to clog up and are durable and there are usually several for sale. Some sellers are very familiar with them, and it's best to get one from a regular seller since they know it works. They also show up on social marketplaces.

Search Words - try different combinations

"Brother" "PocketJet", "Mobile Printer", "Pocket Jet", and the model numbers too, and sort by price. It ranges from $50 to $150. New might be $600.

Models:

PJ-622 PJ-623 PJ-662 PJ-663 PJ-673
PJ-722 PJ-723 PJ-762 PJ-763 ...
PJ-822 PJ-823 PJ-862 PJ-863 ...

You will need a power supply and USB cable, but not a battery, and there are listings on eBay for the right power supplies if it doesn't come with it. Get one that says it works for the printer model number, not just the same voltage and plug. The printers are picky.

The USB cable is easy to get, and you might have one from an old printer, but if the machine does not come with the cable, you may have to shop for it. The connectors change over the years.

Before you buy, make sure the model still works for your computer. See the website "support.brother.com" for the details. Select "Mobile Printers". The Brother website will show which computer operating systems each printer will work with, and has the downloads. The PJ-6xx series is probably the oldest to consider. Ask a techie friend to help if this is new to you.

Printing Stencils

Printing on the PocketJet, the stencil needs a white paper backing; there are optical sensors checking for paper. Cut your thermal material and tape the leading edge glossy side up to a piece of blank white paper the same size. Use clear tape on the leading edge; the trailing edge doesn't need tape.

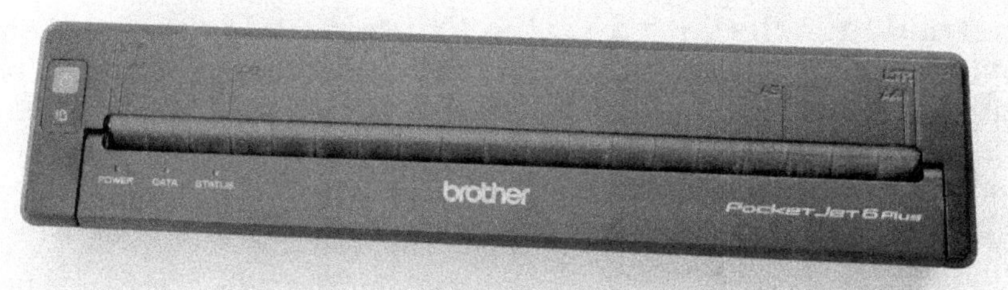

When you are printing from your graphics program to the printer, there will be a screen with some options, like the size paper and portrait or landscape. It takes some fooling with it to get the paper size right, but it's not hard, and you can save the setting. One of the settings will let you change the darkness or density (heat) of the print. You will have to hunt for the exact options. If the stencil art is ragged, it's too hot. If you see just a shadow of the art, it is not hot enough.

Feed the taped leading edge into the slot of the printer glossy side down, making sure it's aligned and *to the right*, not centered. A short press of the feed button will move it forward. I use 4" wide by 8" long for most tumbler stencils and can put two on it.

Print the stencil, and trim off the extra white paper, and you are ready to mark or etch.

For the best quality marking and etching, use 300 DPI, and reverse your art in your graphics program so that when you are etching and marking, the glossy side is down. The glossy surface makes a tighter fit to the metal surface.

I usually roll out 8", cut it, then put it on a sheet of paper and tape the leading edge, then cut the film and paper into a couple of pieces and trim off the excess paper.

The thermal stencil should lay flat on the steel while you are using it since a mark or etch over crinkles is iffy. Trimming helps sometimes.

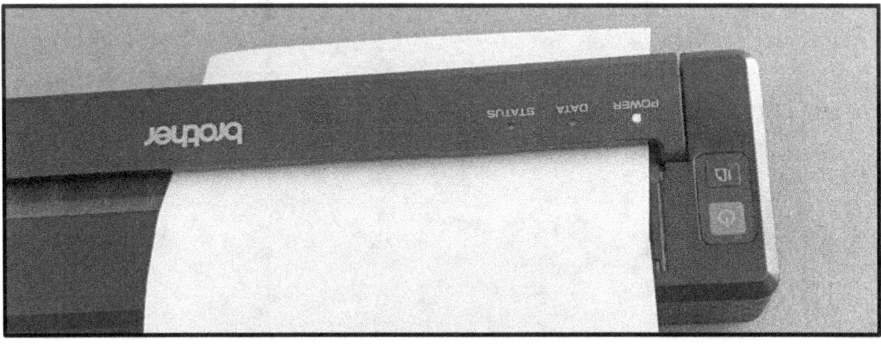

Thermal Stencils with a Tattoo Printer
Some tattoo shops use a thermal printer that is like a copy machine, and it will make thermal stencils for electro etch. It is not connected to a computer, and it reads/copies the artwork from one sheet and thermal prints it. It uses the same thermal paper as the postage printer and the PocketJet. The original art should be on plain white paper.

The thermal copier / tattoo printer I have is similar to *many* others. They all seem to look the same, and cost close to the same from dozens of sellers on Amazon and eBay. About $100 to $150 with free shipping (watch out for extended delivery schedules). There are some new versions, but I have not tested them.

Operation
There are two wide slots, front and back. The front slot takes in the art, and the back slot has a bar that lifts up where you place the thermal paper glossy side down, and snap the bar down.

Cut a piece from your thermal paper roll about 5x8 and a piece of white paper about the same size. Draw something on the white paper with a black pen (fine lines) and a black marker (heavy lines). This is to test the temperature with a few prints to see how it works.

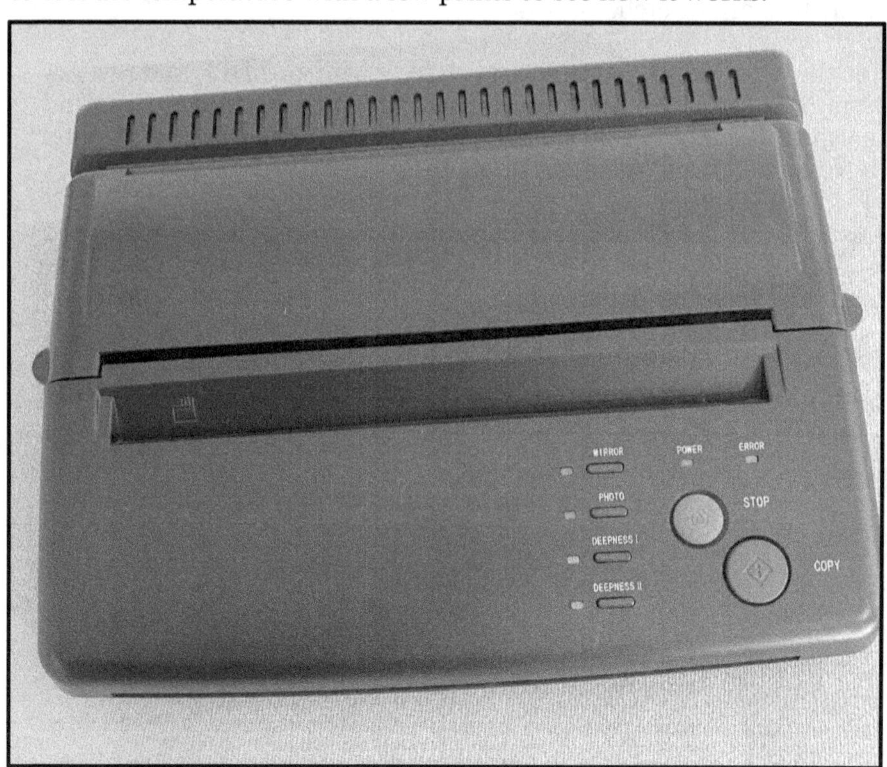

Loading Thermal Paper
The thermal paper is loaded glossy side down and centered. Lift the top bar/flap and place it so the roller presses the glossy surface down on to the thermal strip. No backing paper is needed for this printer.

Loading Artwork
The sheet with art goes forward of it in a slot. Art facing the machine, and mostly lined up with the thermal paper. Both the art and thermal paper are in the center, and there is a little shift of the printing to the thermal off to one side sometimes, and I am not sure exactly when it will do it. Your art and stencil paper can be narrow or wide. It all seems to work but you will have to figure out the alignment.

When you poke the white paper in, the printer will grab it. If it is off kilter, press STOP and it will feed the white paper through so you can position it again. I have not figured out what the other buttons do, except the "photo" which is supposed to be higher resolution. I need to experiment some more with them.

When you push the big button, the art and stencil advance at the same time, and the art is copied and thermally printed. Once you get the alignment figured out, it's excellent. The artwork for this printer does not have to be reversed. The stencil will print so the glossy side is against the metal and the matte side is up while you etch.

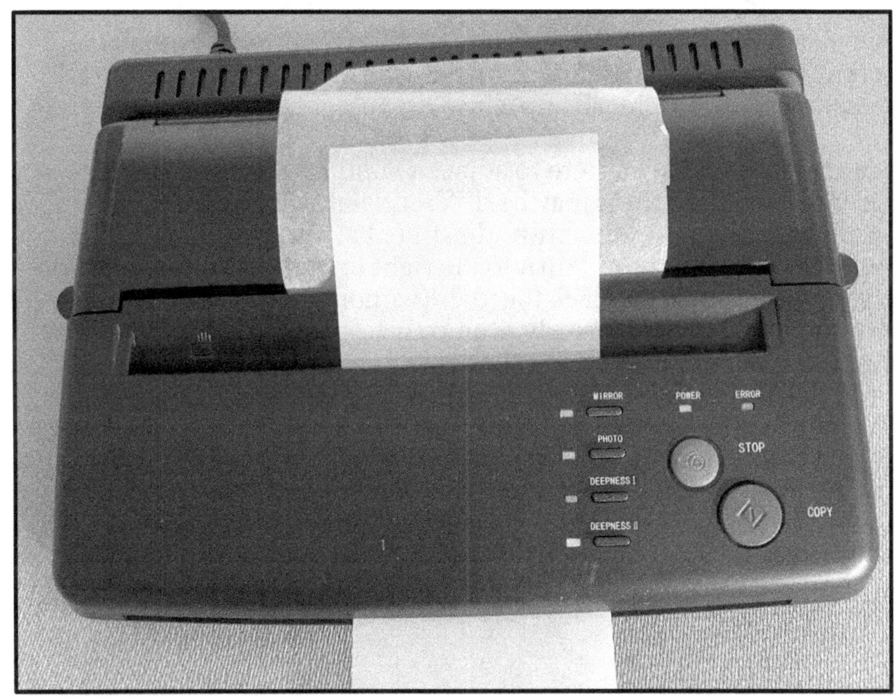

Heat Adjustment of a Tattoo Printer

You may have to open it up to adjust the temperature. See the photos for the adjustment. It's not hard; just four screws on this model. Out of the box, it may be perfect, not hot enough, or too hot. If it is not hot enough, the stencil will have an impression of your art, but not a stencil. Too hot and the edges of the stencil art will be ragged. There is an adjustment screw inside, in the back, so the machine has to be opened up. Unplug it, and remove the power cord. Follow the photos to see where things are. There are a couple of screws holding a plate over where a roll of paper would go, and at the bottom of that space are a couple more screws that are a little longer. Once those are out, flip the machine over, and separate the clam shell halves along the back seam, and as you pry apart the clam about an inch, the circuit board in the back is visible. On my machine, with the rubber feet in the air, the adjustment screw is on the right side, away from the plug.

Don't force any plastic parts. There may be tabs inside. Mine doesn't have them. There is no need to totally separate the halves, all you need is access to a plastic screw on the control board inside at the back. Peek inside, and you should see the circuit board.

There are two ends to the circuit board, and one end hopefully has SECONDARY printed on it, and is the low voltage side that controls the heat. It should be on the other end of the plug connection. The adjustment screw is on the secondary side.

Avoid touching any of the electrical parts except the one adjustment screw. When you are adjusting, make sure the words printed on the circuit board are right side up, since to the right should be hotter.

See the photos to see where to adjust. On my unit, it is an orange screw head. Other units may be different, but will probably be similar. Once you see the little adjustment screw, make a LITTLE turn. Do just a 1/4 or 1/8 turn to the right to make it hotter, or left to make it less hot. Put it back together (without screws) and test it. The parts fit together pretty easily. Run your tests to get the temperature right, and once it's ready, put the screws back.

The tattoo printer / thermal copier makes a good stencil, and it's fast. I don't think the resolution is quite as sharp as the mobile printer, but it's just fine. If you have trouble with it, there are some help videos online, but I have not had any problems that required a reset or anything, just the temperature change.

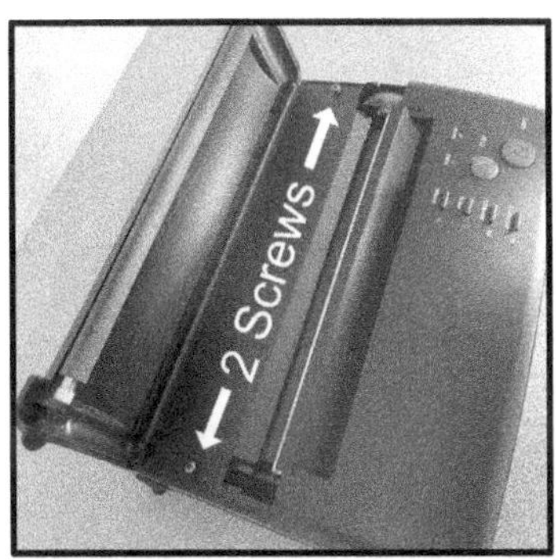

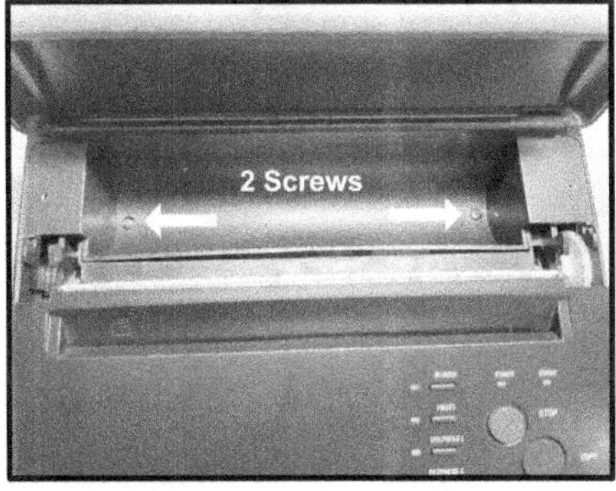

Above: There are 2 screws holding a plate, then 2 screws under that, and the clamshell back should come apart.

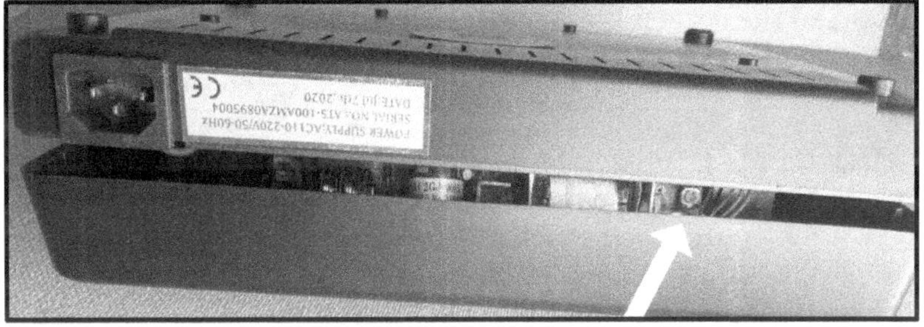

Below: The clamshell is open, and a close up photo shows the adjustment screw. Mine is orange.

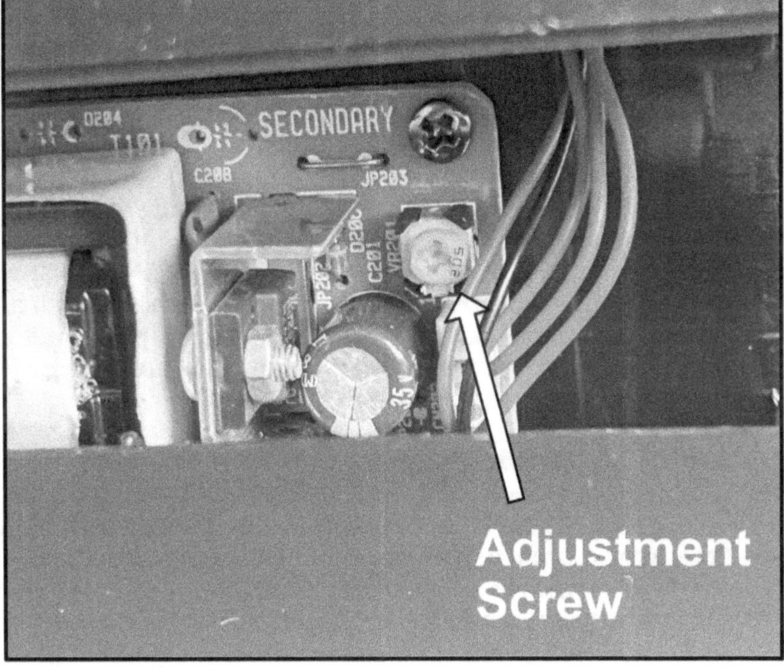

Chapter 12 - Screen Stencils

How to Make Screen Stencils

A screen stencil uses a silkscreen (a very fine poly screen with emulsion) similar to the kind used for printing t-shirts, and is probably the best known electro etch stencil. It is durable, and works for most etching and marking, but I have not found a source for the emulsion, so the screen film is purchased pre-made, then exposed and developed.

Parts
____ Electro Etch Emulsion Screens
____ Clear tape to remove plastic film from screen
____ UV light - purchased or assembled
____ Clear glass that passes UV from old picture frame (4"x6")
____ Black base piece - smooth cardboard painted
____ Matte black acrylic paint $1
____ Developer tray - food to-go tray
____ Old regular toothbrush and a lighter to bend it backwards
____ Soda ash (sodium carbonate), warm water, and container
____ Running water to wash out screen
____ Art that will block light - mask
____ Art Option - Laser or Inkjet on Transparency film
____ Art Option - Cut vinyl
____ Art Option - Printed on white paper and oiled
____ Art Option - Drawn with black ink on transparency film
____ Timer - to measure seconds

The emulsion is a light sensitive coating that is UV exposed with a mask (your art), developed, and washed out. If you only need a few stencils, it's easier to order them custom made. They are durable if you control the heat and take care of them.

Custom Screen Stencils
Order custom screen stencils from knife makers and outfits that sell electro etching supplies and make custom electro etch stencils. After you send them the art and explain how many versions and sizes you need, they will work with you to get your art ready for a stencil. Give your stencils some room around them so you don't have to tape

around them as much. Ask the seller how to care for them too. Before you order, make sure they are selling stencils for electro etching - if they don't know, chances are it won't work. Most screen emulsions don't work for electro etching.

Making Screen Stencils
You can make your own screen stencils if you buy the stencil film. It is usually sold as 4"x4" sheets or as 8"x10" sheets. They have a protective layer of clear mylar plastic film on each side, and are delivered in a light-proof foil envelope. When you order, make sure it's not an impact stencil, and make sure it will work for electro etch. If the store/seller isn't sure about the electro etch part, then it probably won't work. See www.electroetchdiy.com for some sellers.

Low Light Work Area
The work area should be low light - at least no bright light coming in. It does not have to be dark like for photography, but low light is important. Maybe avoid the time of day when sunlight comes into the room. Some stencil material may be more sensitive. Ask the seller. I used to do it in the dark, but it's just not that touchy.

Keep your screen in the light proof packet until you are ready to cut it and use it. Find a dark corner in the room to open the foil packet, pull out a sheet, cut it up, then put everything back in the foil pack except what you will be using, and cover that piece to reduce light exposure. Keep the packet reasonably cool. Don't leave it in the car.

Art Mask
A screen stencil is exposed in UV light with a light blocking (a mask) version of your art placed closely over the screen to prevent light getting to the emulsion underneath. The blocked off emulsion does not cure and is washed/scrubbed out in the developer and rinse. Your art must block light. If it lets UV through, then those parts of the stencil will cure and not wash out, and will and not be part of the etch.

Transparency Film
You can print your art on clear transparency film sold at office stores for laser or inkjet. Use black ink, print it, then cut it down to size. Place it printed side down against the screen stencil, then lay the glass down over it to hold it flat as you expose it. Sometimes stacking two copies will help if it's not dark enough.

White Paper and Oil
You can print your art on white copy paper and cut it down to size, and then oil it to make it translucent. Use a light oil like canola oil or WD-40 oil. Lay it into position, ink side down, right on the film and

it's plastic layer, and wipe up any extra oil and remove any bubbles. Don't lay the glass on it, since it should lay flat. Exposure is about 20 seconds with UV LED, but it will take testing it to get it right.

Ink
Some inks will write on transparency films and can make stencils. I've used a black ink from Rapidograph called India Ink "Universal 3080F.BLA". It dries quickly and blocks light. It comes in a bottle, and is used with a technical pen or a dip pen.

Vinyl
Dark vinyl works as a mask. Cut it and transfer it to transparency film and use it vinyl side down on the screen stencil.

Brush
I use an old regular toothbrush that I've heated and bent the head back over. The head in that position can brush the stencil while it is flat in the tray. Use it gently till you get the hang of the developer process.

Developer Solution
After exposure, the screen is developed in an alkali solution, where you brush and cajole the goo out from the threads. You can buy developer or make it.

Developer Neutralizer Solution
After the developer and rinse steps, the stencil may still be kind of slimy. A few drops of citric acid solutions eliminates the slime, and make the stencil much less sticky. A slimy stencil will stick to things while it dries and can be ruined.

Developer Solution Recipe
_____ ¼ tsp Soda Ash, also called Sodium Carbonate or Washing Soda
_____ 4 oz Warm Water
_____ pH about 11

Neutralizer Solution Recipe
_____ ¼ tsp Citric Acid
_____ 4 oz Warm Water
_____ pH is about 2

Soda ash is used in cleaning products and tie-dye. This concentration is about as harsh as many cleaners. If your hands are sensitive, or you are doing many, use gloves. It is not heated before using. Citric acid is found in the canning area of the grocery near the mason jars. Some stencils may require a special developer.

Tape

Have a piece of tape ready for the thin film peel step. The stencil has a super thin layer of plastic on each side, and a piece of clear tape works well to grab it and remove it. I use the piece of tape on a corner to catch it and peel it off, then do the other side.

UV Light

Making screen stencils uses UV light to expose the emulsion. I experimented for years with different lights. Screen print bulbs, Reptile lights, CFL tubes, CFL floods, ... UVC bulbs. I get the best results from a panel of UV LED. You can buy or make one from UV LED strips.

Buying a UV Panel

Making screen stencils requires UV light exposure. A UV panel with LED will expose stencil film. Make sure the panel light is in the range of 395nm to 405nm. It might be one number or a range. If it just says purple or black light, get a different one. It's kind of hard to know exactly which one to get, but for tumbler size (4" x 6" stencil film) a 10W will work. A higher watt unit would be better for larger exposures. Hold the light over white paper, and find the height where the light is pretty even, and covers the size film you are exposing or more. You will need to do some tests with the screen material and light panel to find the height and time where it all works. You can prop the panel up with something, but holding it for 10 or 20 seconds is not hard, and movement of the light makes no difference. The panels cost $20 and up on Amazon. The 10W with 395nm LED by Everbeam is about $20.

Making a UV Panel

You can buy a roll of 5V LED in the same 395nm range, and make your own with some soldering; just get one that is not waterproof, and runs on 5V with a USB plug. Each group of LED between the copper nubs is a working piece, so you can cut it up at the nubs and solder them together on a panel.

Black Base Sheet

The base under the screen while exposing is flat, non-reflective, and black. You can use a postcard, a piece of hardboard, or most anything smooth, and paint it matte black. I paint it with $1 matte black acrylic from the craft aisle and a paper towel brush. It works better than foam I used to use, and does not need clamps.

Glass Sheet

A glass sheet from small picture frame - tested to pass UV. Shine your UV panel in the closet at clothing (some will glow) through the sheet - no glow - no go. Some glass will block UV and won't work.

Exposing the Stencil

To set up for exposure, build layers like a parfait; or like an onion if you prefer.

The "Base Sheet" layer is the smooth matte black surface
On top of that is "Stencil Screen", plastic film still in place
On top of that is "Art Mask". Ink side down on the film
On top of that is "Glass Sheet" - no glass needed for the oil on paper
Put about ¼" of developer in a shallow tray

Place your UV panel over the sandwich a few inches above it so the lights blur and individual dots are no longer visible, and turn it on for 15 seconds (20 to 30 seconds for oil paper). Prop it up with LEGO or something, or just hold it. See the photos in a few pages.

The Peel

After exposure, remove the glass, and art, and remove the screen off the black base. Use tape to grip and peel the thin film off each side; it's better than a fingernail.

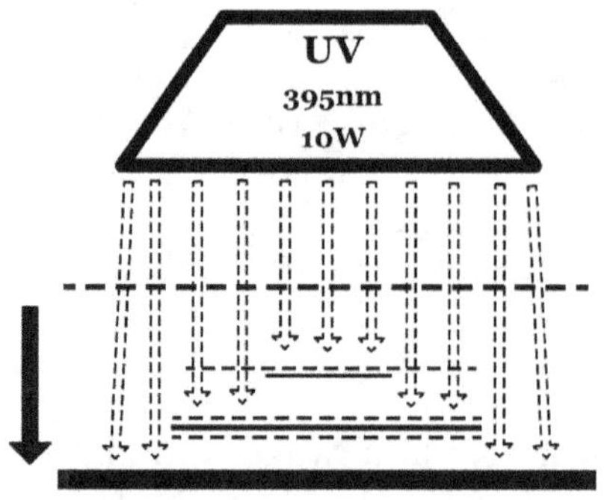

Develop Stencil

Put the exposed screen in the developer. Swirl it around for a few seconds, then gently start brushing with the toothbrush, and swirl some more. You should be able to see your art in the screen while you brush in all directions. Do this for a couple of minutes, flipping it over often so you are doing both sides. You can feel the art on the screen. If you leave the screen in for a few minutes longer, the non-art part will soften too. It takes practice to dial in, but two minutes is a good start. If you are developing more than one stencil, keep them separated since they will stick to each other.

Emulsion is Goo

Knowing that the unexposed emulsion is SOFTENED is important. Most of it must be brushed and cajoled and sprayed out from between the tiny threads; it is not all dissolved. Once it's mostly out, it's hard to see if there is a thin layer still in place.

The Wash

Rinse the film under a faucet, trying to make the water push through the art pattern and clean out the bits of goo. Hold it at the bottom of the water stream to get more force. Hold the stencil up to light, and you should be able to see that it's cleaned out. For small details, it can be very hard to tell.

Neutralizer

The developer is pretty basic (pH of 11) and the screen emulsion will feel slimy. A few drops of the citric acid (pH of 2) and quick rinse will take the slime away.

Stencil Test

Before you start etching with your stencil on something important, look carefully to make sure all the parts washed out. If all the parts of the art are not clean, try rinsing again, and if that doesn't work, put it back in the developer and scrub a few seconds, and then rinse again. Once you think it's washed out, use the stencil to mark some test steel to make sure all the parts show up.

Problems

Not blocking enough light with the art mask is a common problem. It has to block the light or it cures what is under it, and that part of the screen does not wash out. Not cajoling all the goo from between the threads is also a common problem, and not rinsing long enough can leave thin translucent emulsion between the threads.

Extra Cure

Once I know the screen stencil is good, I put it under the UV panel another 10 seconds. This will cure it some more.

Stencil Care

After you etch, wash the stencil in water, and lay it on paper to dry before you store it. If you lay it on glass or plastic, it might stick and ruin it. Be careful with tape since it can remove emulsion too. Store them out of the light and separated if they are sticky at all.

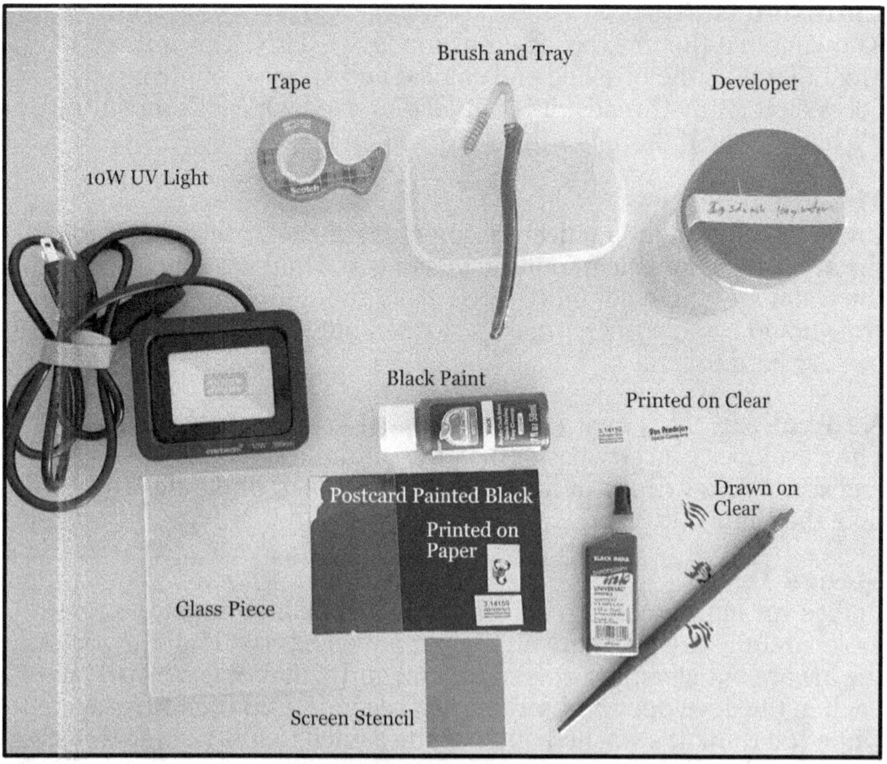

Tape
Brush and Tray
Developer
10W UV Light
Black Paint
Printed on Clear
Drawn on
Clear
Postcard Painted Black
Printed on
Paper
Glass Piece
Screen Stencil

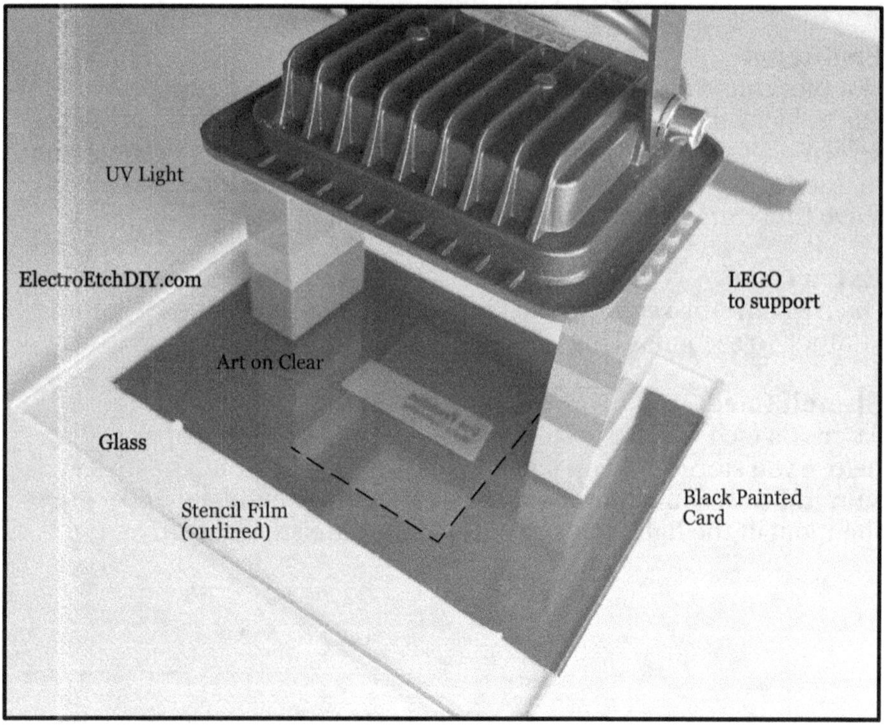

UV Light
ElectroEtchDIY.com
LEGO
to support
Art on Clear
Glass
Stencil Film
(outlined)
Black Painted
Card

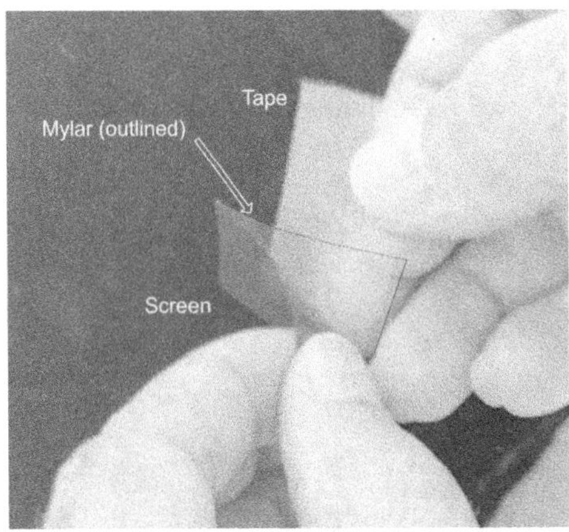

Above: Removing the mylar from each side with a piece of tape after 15 to 20 seconds of exposure to UV.

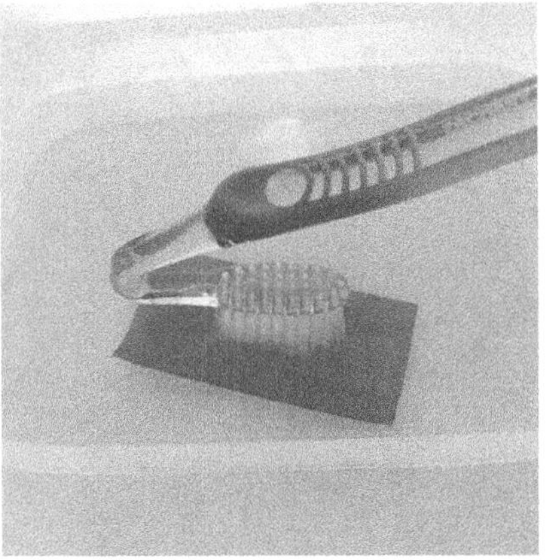

Above: Firmly brush, flip, and brush, flip for 2 minutes or so, then wash under the faucet.

Below: A very close look at a screen stencil. The cutout from the left edge of a five dollar bill is a good size comparison.

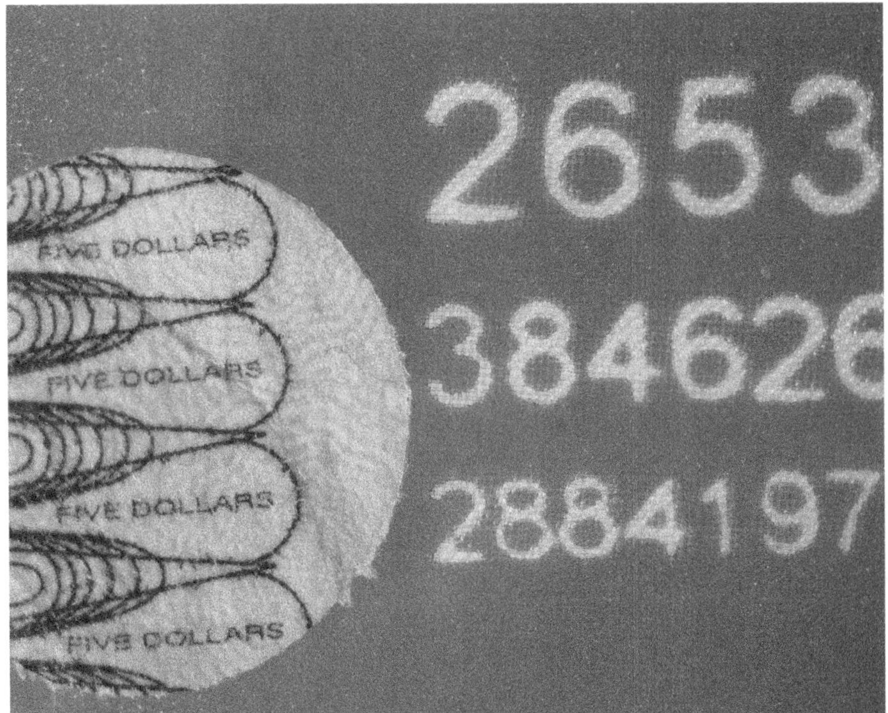

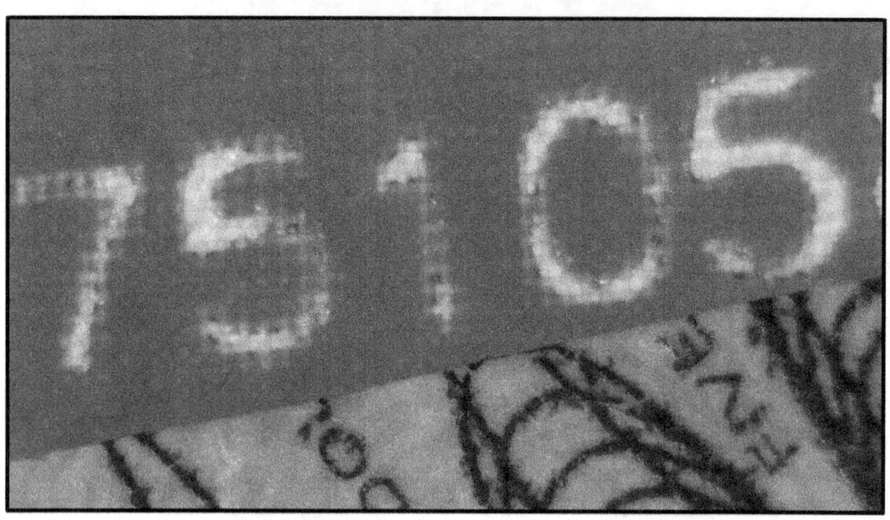

Above: Stencils are a fine woven poly, and sometimes the emulsion does not clean out completely. Usually from art not blocking UV.

Below: Taping a stencil on both ends helps keep things from moving around. This is Scotch brand blue painters tape holding it down.

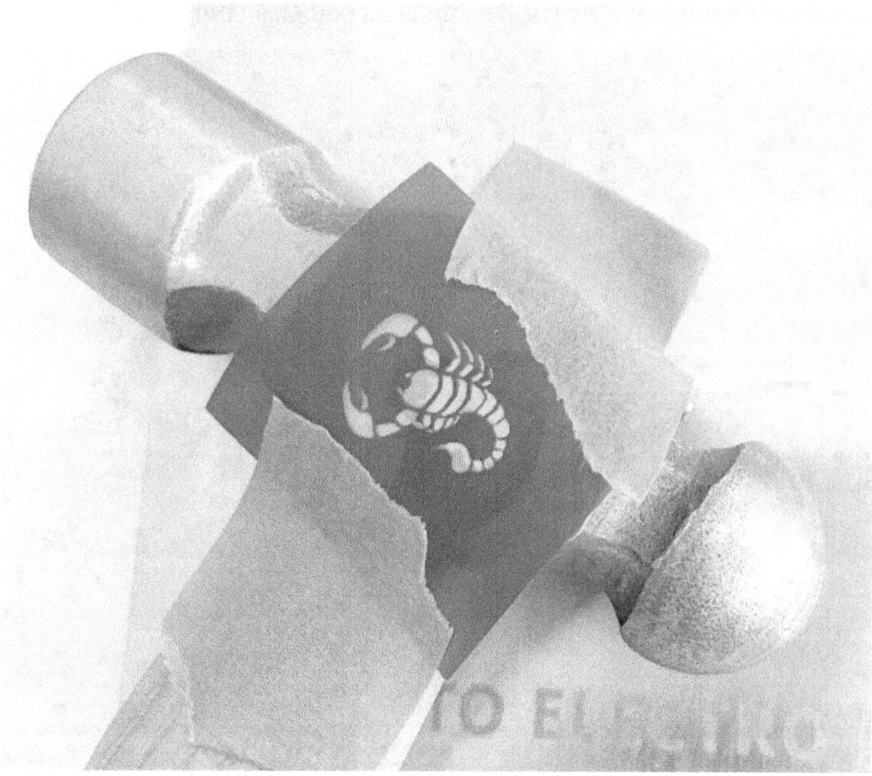

Practice the Exposure, Develop, and Rinse

You will need to experiment to dial in the time, and practice developing. Cut four small pieces of stencil film about half inch by an inch, and cover half of each one with black tape. Expose the first one for 10 seconds, peel it, develop it, and wash it out. Do it again with a 15 second exposure, then a 20 second, then a 30 second. Then leave a developed one in the developer for longer until the exposed emulsion breaks down.

Stencil Emulsion is Goo

Scrubbing the stencil out while it's in the developer and then rinsing the screen under the faucet seems like an easy process, but it is very tricky to get all the goo out. Sometimes it's blocked and hard to see. The stencil below is good. The screen does not have blockages. If the art does not block enough UV, the emulsion will not wash out.

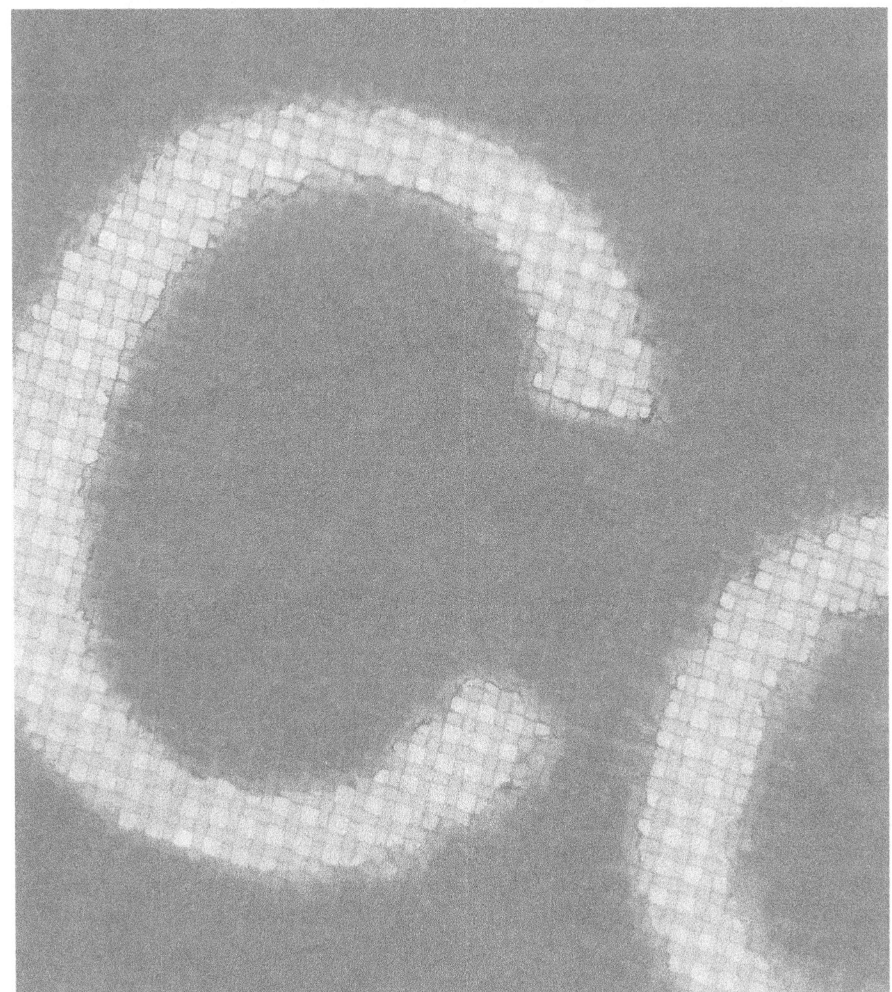

Chapter 13 - Electro Etching

How to Electro Etch

Once you have an etching machine, it is time to make sure it works by doing an etch, a mark, and an etch followed by a mark. The steps and problem solving are the same for all kinds of steel.

Make an Etch and a Mark
Knowing that a machine will work for an etch and for a mark is a good starting place. We can do that even before we have real stencils.

Parts and Supplies
Electro etch machine that will etch with DC and mark with AC, along with the base plate, handpiece, felt pads, graphite, and electrolyte.

Test Supplies
A test stencil is made of electrical tape or Scotch blue painters tape with holes punched into it. Lay it on wax paper and use a hole punch to make three holes in it. For the test steel, the thrift stores have a bunch of good stuff; old flatware, pots, and pans are good if they are stainless. Feeler gauges (they look like a peacock tail fanned out) are excellent to practice on, and are about $6, with high quality carbon steel; unbolt it, and practice with the leaves. Oil them to reduce rusting, and sand them down to practice on them again. Your kitchen drawers have lots of steel. Don't use a fancy 304 steel for this test.

Regular Supplies
Paper towels, scissors to cut stencils and pads (cut up), gloves, a plastic quart bag to lay wet handpiece on, a tray to work over to protect your table, and polishing supplies. I use Mother's Mag and Aluminum polish with cotton swabs, or a Sandflex block with fine grit, and sometimes 400 grit sandpaper called 3M Pro Grade No Slip. For setting up the etch, I use clear tape, or Scotch blue painters tape, or my new favorite, Elmer's Re-Stick Glue stick. Just lay it on the stencil and place your stencil on the steel. You can pick up and move it, then, once you are finished, use it again on the next etch. It will wash off of the steel and out of the stencil. A multimeter is good to have to fix problems. For less than $10 it will measure volts and resistance.

Setting Up

Pre-Etch Check
- Make sure you are using a clean pad
- Etching needs a thicker material than marking
- Handpiece should be flat on its working surface
- If handpiece is crusty, wipe the salts off with a wet paper towel
- A clamp that's not too rusty where it holds the handpiece
- The stencil is not blocked by gunk
- Electrical connections are all tight (they loosen by magic)
- The workpiece wire is on the lug for an etch or mark
- The metal to be etched is not coated with anything

A dry, fouled, or partly wet pad can make it seem like things are not working, and a loose wire or crusty clamp or salty graphite block will too. An uneven handpiece working surface can interfere with a good mark or etch. If your pad is dried out from the last session, and you just wet it again, there may be salt crystals between the pad and handpiece that cause problems.

Felt and Electrolyte
Cut a piece of felt, and rubber band it to your graphite handpiece; it should cover the end of the graphite. Clamp your handpiece to it. Drip some saltwater vinegar on the pad; the first drop might not break and absorb, but add some more and it will, then saturate the pad. Blot on a paper towel if drippy.

Simple Stencil - Three Holes
Make three holes in a piece of vinyl electrical tape or Scotch blue painters tape (on wax paper) with a paper punch, or Xacto and place the tape on a feeler gauge or dinner knife or test steel. We will do an etch, a mark, then an etch followed by a mark.

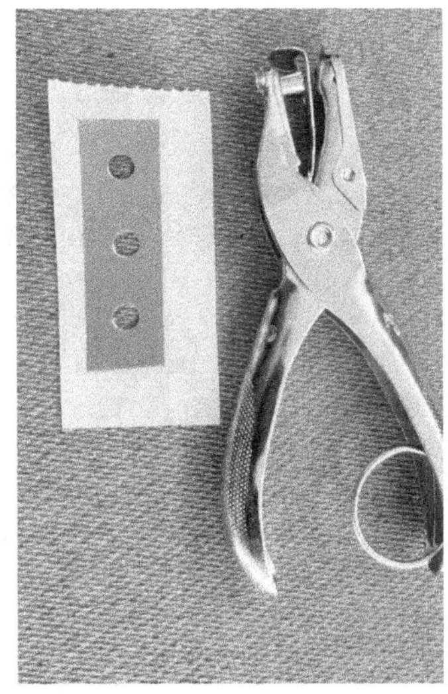

Setting Up
Make sure you can easily power on and off your machine. Leave it off for now. The base plate should have the workpiece wire alligator clip on it, and the handpiece clamp has your graphite with wet pad. With a larger graphite block, you might need to space out the holes.

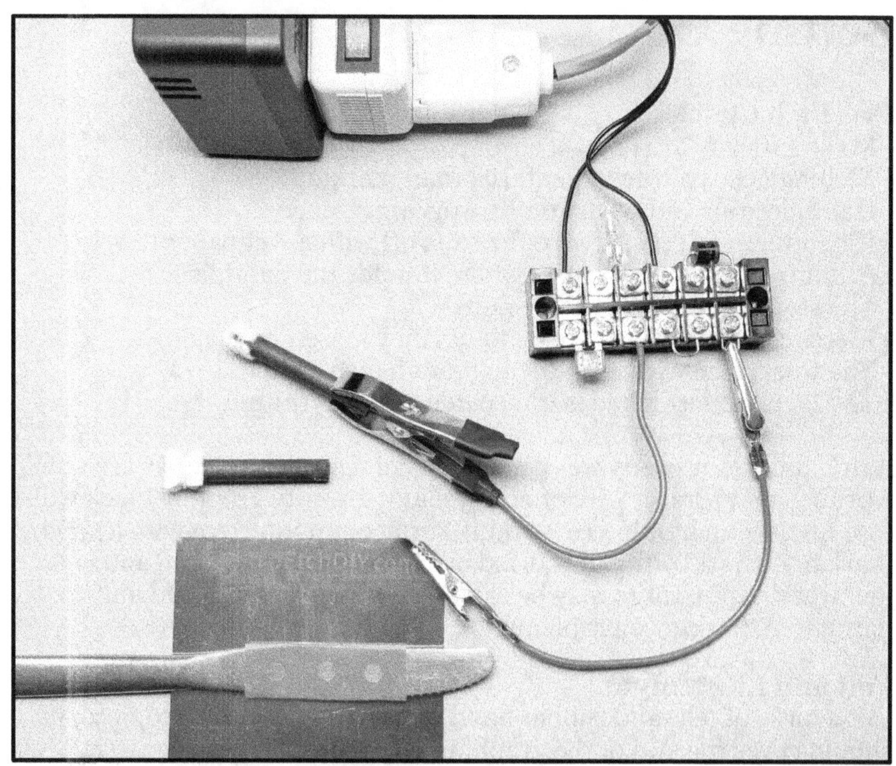

Marking and Etching Practice

Making an Etch

Connect the workpiece wire alligator clip to the ETCH lug ("+" positive) on your machine and power on the machine. The 6th lug.

Place and hold the handpiece with wet felt on the first hole for several seconds and lift, then repeat several times, making sure to get the whole thing. As you do this, the resistor / bulb will warm up, and there should be bubbling at the pad as it progresses. The pad will start turning dark then gunky. You might also smell chlorine gas - it smells like a hotel swimming pool. Best not to inhale it.

Do this for a minute or more. Lifting the handpiece releases gasses that form which is needed for other kinds of stencils but also repositions the felt and makes the etch more even. The etch may be black with oxides on some steels, but it is not durable black like a mark. With thermal stencils and screen stencils, a halo or haze is common. It will polish out with Mother's Mag and Aluminum polish or fine sandpaper. Blot the etch with a paper towel to remove extra electrolyte, and prepare for a mark.

Making a Mark

Turn off the machine, and replace the pad, and wet it with electrolyte again. When you are removing the old pad, watch for tiny drops the snappy rubber band sends out - they stain clothing.

Move the workpiece wire alligator clip to the MARK lug (#4 & #5) and turn on the machine. The mark always uses low voltage AC.

On the second hole, dab and hold the handpiece over it a few times. A mark is much faster than an etch. A mark is a dark oxide layer you might barely be able to feel it, but you can always see it. Sometimes holding it down longer will make it darker. The pad does not get as gunky, and can be used for the next etch. Work it for a little while, and it should give you a good mark.

Etch then Mark

A common method is to make an etch, then mark it to darken it. The oxide inside the adds contrast. On the third stencil, with the same pad, do an etch followed by a mark.

Move the workpiece wire to the ETCH lug. Wet the felt if needed, then etch the third hole for a minute or two, then then move the workpiece wire to the MARK lug, and mark it for several seconds. You don't need to power down when you move the alligator clip, just unclip it and move it. If your hands are wet, use gloves.

Checking the Results

Peel the tape off the three holes, and dab some ammonia neutralizer on them if you are using carbon steel, then scrub with a moist paper towel. You should have an etch you can see and feel, a dark mark, and an etch you can feel that is dark inside. Steels that are fast to rust should be dried and oiled. If you don't have a good etch and mark, there is a problem somewhere; step through the list in the next pages for problem solving.

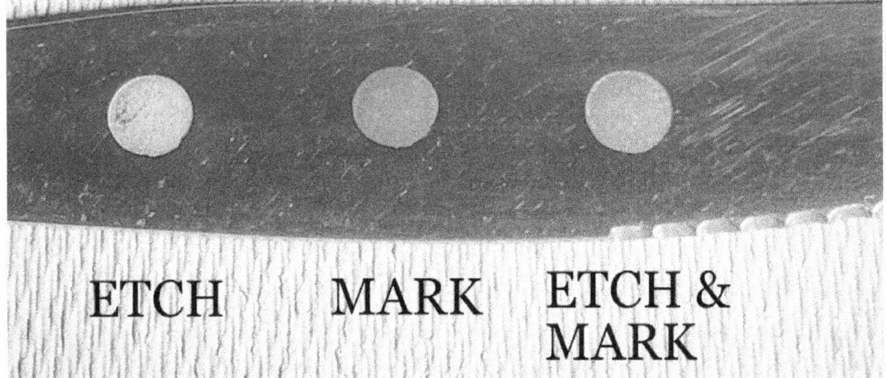

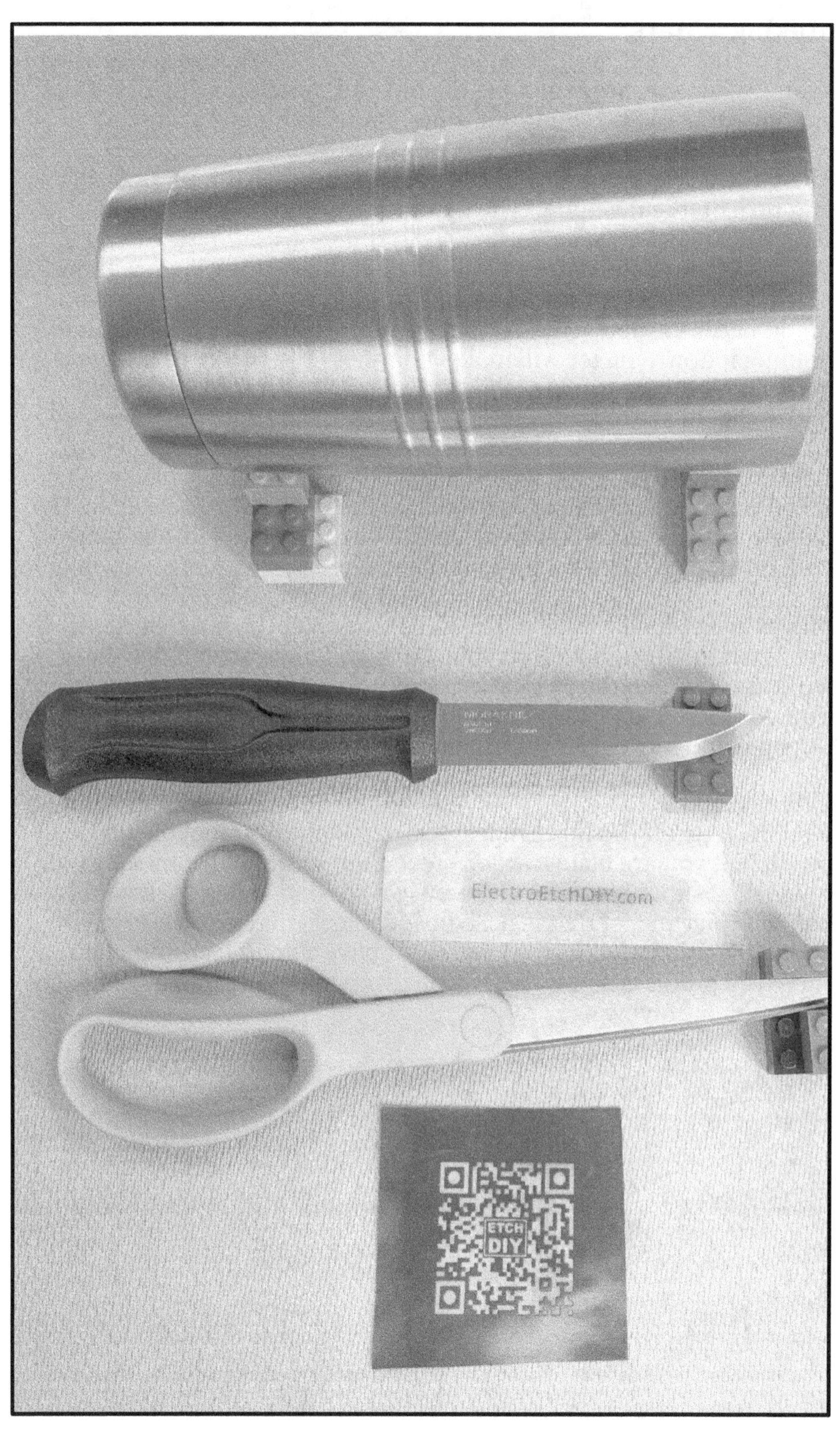
ElectroEtchDIY.com
ETCH
DIY

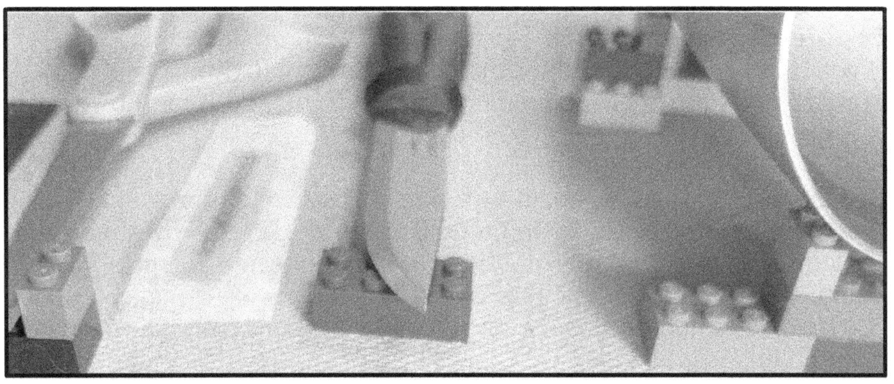

Supporting & Taping

When I am electro etching odd shapes, it helps to have them supported so they don't wiggle quite as much. The supports don't need to be immovable, they just need to provide an easy non-metal support. If you don't have to think about the support while etching or marking, it's easier.

Cover any exposed metal the handpiece pad might hit, so it doesn't etch where it shouldn't. Smaller handpieces might work better sometimes. Scotch tape - either the clear or the blue painters works great, and many others do too. Fold an end to make a tab so you can lift it off without having to pick at it.

Taped down stencil protecting the metal
from the handpiece pad that is kind of large.

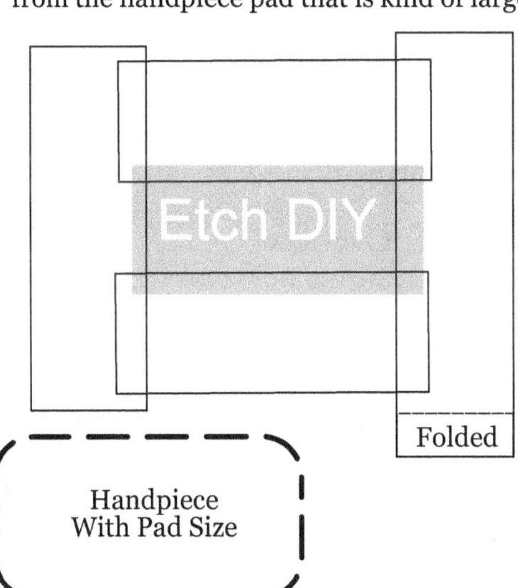

Problem Solving

If you don't get a good etch or mark, here are some things to check. Make sure all the lugs and connections are tight, and it has power. If your switch tap has a light when it's on, it helps.

Did the bulb or resistor warm up while you were etching? If not, touch the handpiece clamp to the end of the workpiece clip, and if the resistor does not heat up, something is not connected correctly. Is the bulb intact and 12V? Is the fuse good? If you measure voltage, on the mark lug it should be close or over the full amount, and half that on the etch lug.

If the the resistor warmed up when you touched the handpiece clamp to the workpiece clip, then touch the handpiece clamp to the knife surface. The resistor should heat up; if not, is the steel anodized or coated? It has to pass electricity.

Was the etch too shallow to feel? Make sure the workpiece wire was on the etch lug on the far right, and the diode stripe is to the right. If not, it won't etch.

Was the mark dark enough? Make sure your workpiece wire is attached to the mark lug. Are you using the salt and vinegar or the baking soda? Are you using at least 6V? And AC? There is an organic look to a mark with a darkness variation.

Did the pad get gunky like it's supposed to for an etch? Did you use one of the suggested electrolytes? Did you use a felt pad, or some layers of padding? If you used a thin pad, you might not have gotten much of an etch before it clogs up. Was the pad wet enough? A dry pad or crusty graphite will not do much and is splotchy.

If you are using a screen stencil, is it clean enough to pass electrolyte everywhere under the artwork, and it is all open where it should be?

Handpiece and Direct Action

The handpiece and pad have to be worked over each part of the stencil, or parts of the art will be left out. The etch or mark does not spread very much and it's stronger under the handpiece than under the pad that extends around it. Protect areas around your stencil, since the pad will etch or mark if it goes past the stencil, and a dribble of electrolyte can cause a dribble mark. Go up and down on the stencil or go down then roll, instead of sliding and rubbing; it less damaging to the stencil, and it keeps the stencil from shifting.

Durability Test
Rub the mark, etch, and etch/mark down with a cloth, and scrub it with kitchen scrubby pads, and other cleaning supplies. They are durable. Metal polish or abrasives will fade out a mark but do not affect an etch. Now sand the mark until it goes away. First the oxide will come off, and a very light etch remains, then it will sand off. Do the same for the etch - it will take a while. In day to day use, the mark or etch are very long lasting, but a mark will polish off if it's on a keychain or pet tag rubbing up against other metal.

Special Steels
Some steels don't work well with saltwater, but store bought electrolyte is available for all of them.

Plated Metals
If the metal is plated with chrome or nickel, use the saltwater and vinegar mix, and only do a mark. There are also special electrolytes available for plated metals. If you etch on plated metal, it will probably remove the plating and may expose copper under it.

Coated Metal
If your metal has a coating, even if it's conductive, it may not etch or mark properly. Some coatings are clear, and you can't easily tell they are preventing an etch. If it has a lacquer you might be able to poke it gently with a pin and see the coating. If it's anodized, it can be hard to tell without testing it with a multimeter - the setting is called continuity, and usually there is a symbol for sound / bell.

Surface Finish
A mark is great on brushed steel tumblers. Knives may be high polish, bead blast, brushed, an oxide or a specialty finish. I have not tried Damascus. If you are making a knife, you can etch and clean up the halo. If you are working on surfaces you can't clean up, use a mark, or very short etch.

Stencil Placement
The stencil should be flat on the steel. If your stencil is right up against something that keeps it from being flat, trim it so it will lay flat if possible. If there are curves in two directions - sideways on a tumbler, then a curve down, it can be tricky to make the stencil lay flat enough since it can wrinkle.

Stencil Movement
If the stencil moves even a tiny bit while etching or marking it messes it up with a double mark or etch. Holding it still is really important, and lifting to look almost never works.

Tape To Hold Things and Mask
Scotch clear tape or Scotch blue painters tape will hold things down and mask around the stencil to prevent the handpiece from marking or etching where it shouldn't. When taping a stencil, the tape may strip off part of the stencil surface, so plan where to place tape if you will use the stencil again. The Elmer's Re-Stick is great too, and will wash out of a stencil if you clean it up after your etching.

Capillary Etch
Be careful with where you lay down tape that protects your steel. Using tape to control where an etch goes can make tiny sharp lines where two pieces of tape overlap if they are on the steel. Try and start the overlap over the stencil. The microscopic gaps suck electrolyte in and can etch a thin line.

Under Creep
Avoid letting electrolyte creep between your steel and the base plate, since it will foul the underside. Blotting a soppy pad on a paper towel helps prevent that, and the right size handpiece too.

Unexpected Marks / Pits
If there are shadows, dots or darkening where there shouldn't be, your stencil is passing electricity in those areas. If the stencil is good for electro etching, then dots are from more voltage and amps than the stencil can handle, or a stencil used too many times, or the artwork had dots. If your etching machine does not have a resistor, it can allow more power and heat than the stencil can handle.

Non-Insulating Stencil
Some stencils look like they will work, but are not insulators, and will not protect the surface from electricity. When that happens, there will be marks, blotches, or etches in unexpected places under the stencil. If you see an outline of your stencil on the steel, it's not a fully insulating material. If it's a very mild outline, it may sand out.

Experiment with Etching Power
Trying out different amps (power) is useful - you can get different results with different amps, up to the limit of what your power source and stencils are happy with. The etching machine resistor is easy to change out so you can experiment.

Experiment with Pads
Try marking with a thin pad like a piece of cotton shirt. A mark works well with a thin pad. Now do an etch with that pad and a stencil. The amps will go higher than with a felt pad. The thin pad will foul very quickly, and gunk up the stencil too. Try doubling or tripling a thin pad so it can absorb more oxides.

Deeper Etching

If you are going for a deeper etch, there are things to watch. The stencil has to handle the heat, the pad has to be wet enough, or have electrolyte added, and the pad has to absorb the gunk and get changed out before it fouls the stencil. The saltwater and baking soda electrolyte does not foul the stencil and steel nearly as quickly as the saltwater and vinegar. For production deep etching, a commercial electrolyte will make sense. They have solved most of the problems with fouling.

Handpiece Movement

It helps to move the handpiece and pad around to lots of different places on the stencil as you etch and mark, since it makes things more even. If you don't move the pad, you might see raised areas inside the etch and even some patterns in the steel from the fibers in the pad.

Oiling or Wetting

For stencil etching, a tiny bit of oil on the metal improves the etch - it is a little more crisp. Oil like "3 in One", or "WD-40" work, and others. Rub the oil on, then place the stencil and run your finger over the artwork and stencil to smooth it out. The stencil does not have to be dry underneath. You can also wet the metal with electrolyte, lay the stencil down, smooth it, and etch or mark. The electricity and action will stay where the stencil open parts are, and does not run under the other parts, except for a tiny amount around the edges, creating a halo or haze. At very low voltage, it will slow things down. Oil used with mark tends to make the oxide layer gray or less black.

Halo, Haze & Fuzz

This is a biggie. After etching with most stencils, there may be a haze or halo around the edges of the etch. Before you grab the sandpaper, try the polish. Mother's Mag and Aluminum Polish and cotton swabs will usually remove the halo. Try a few longer deep etches for practice with a thermal or screen stencil, then remove the haze. Vinyl stencils have sticky edges so you may not get the halo or very little. There is a 3M version of sandpaper I like that has a backing on it that is grippy. They call it 3M Pro Grade No Slip, and it's purple. The grit I use is 400 and sand in the direction of the existing finish on tumblers. There is a rubber eraser sanding block called Sandflex (fine) I like.

Disposal

Once the etch pad is saturated with oxides, I put it in the trash. Don't rinse the pads in the sink, since there are all sorts of metals in it.

Electro Etch a Tumbler

Decorating a tumbler is easy. Stainless steel tumblers are great for larger marking and smaller etching. As long as it is not coated, painted, or anodized, it can be decorated with electro etching. A mark will stand out more on tumblers and jugs than an etch, but an etch can be very nice for smaller art. Try larger etches and see if you like the effect. It will depend a lot on the art. Vinyl, screen, and thermal stencils work well.

Practice First
The craft stores and Harbor Freight sell cheap stainless tumblers, and you can sand off a mark over and over as you practice. Once you get the hang of aligning things, the high dollar brand name tumblers work the same way. The Harbor Freight tumblers I use hold heat as well as tumblers that cost five times more.

Organic Art
Tumblers decorated with a mark have an organic feel to them. The oxide is not 100% the same across the mark, and the color ranges from very dark brown to gray depending on the steel, the voltage, and the electrolyte. It is part of the beauty.

Electrolyte
Saltwater or saltwater with vinegar works for most tumblers. I have not hit on a tumbler that would not mark. Blot the handpiece before you start so you don't get get streaks. If a drip slides down off the stencil, it might leave a trail.

Attach the Stencil
Tear off a couple of inches of tape, and fold a little bit of one end over as a tab, then line up the stencil on the tumbler. You can hold the other side while you mark, or tape it down. It takes practice and good light to line up a thermal stencil. The Elmer's Re-Stick applied to the whole stencil does a good job holding the stencil too.

Tumbler Curves
On lots of steel, you have a big flat area the stencil will lay flat on. On some, it is flat for a few inches, then curves. If the stencil does not lay flat, it will be hard to do nice work. Curves in one direction are fine, but curves in two directions make a crinkle.

Reverse Art
The thermal stencil should be printed so that the matte side is facing up when you are using it. The art will be crisper with the glossy side down.

Workpiece Wire
I usually attach the alligator clip to the lip of the tumbler.

Erasing a Mark
If you moved the stencil or it was not aligned and you need to start over, you can sandpaper off the old mark. Most tumblers are not high polish, so you can sand in the direction of the existing finish. At first the oxide will come off, then sand until the shadow goes away. Sandpaper or a Sandflex block works. Be patient with it.

Each part of the art needs to be dabbed over several times, and you can see which parts need more attention. Don't forget the very edges of the art. Sometimes they get left out.

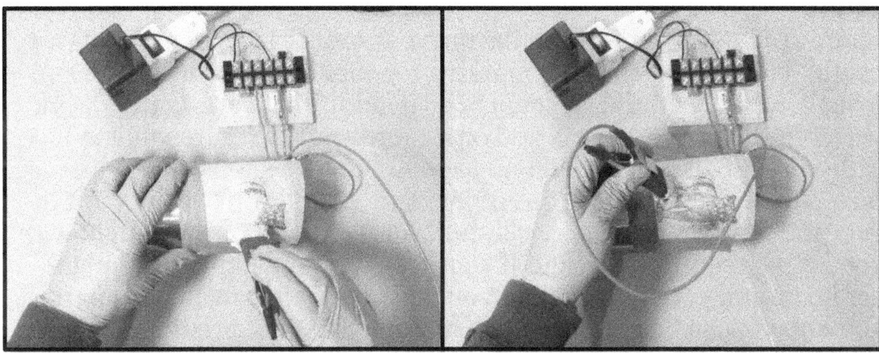

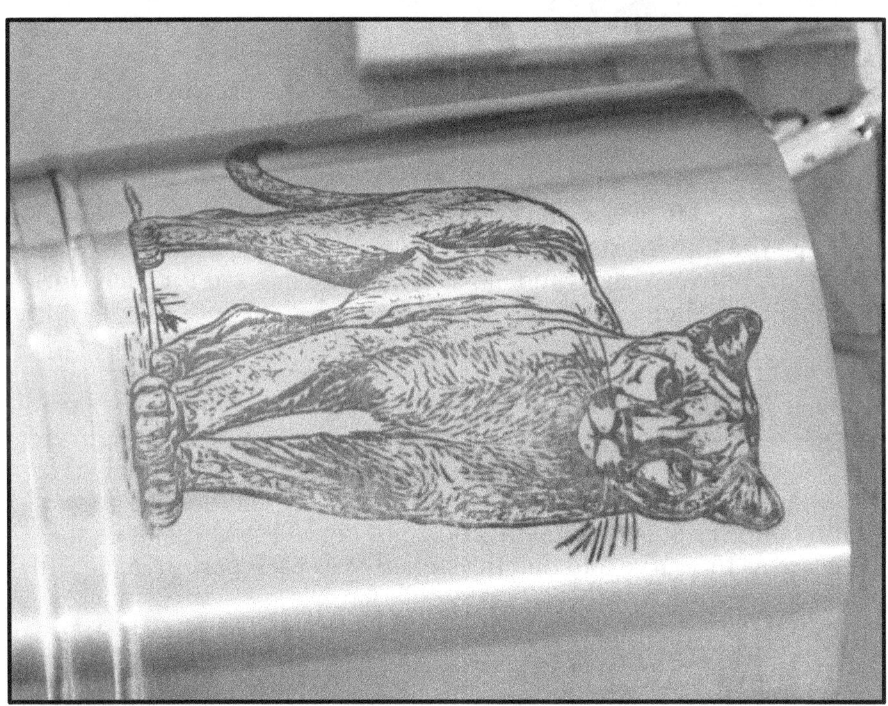

Electro Etch Your Tools

Marking and etching your tools is easy, and tool companies have used electro etching for decades for logos, serial numbers, and quality control marks.

Making History
Some tools end up being passed to family, friends, and coworkers, and are cherished. An etch or mark is a pretty neat reminder of it's history; I think old tools are magical, and those old initials or symbols are neat. Someday a grandkid will pull out a tool with initials etched into it, and there will be a story to tell.

Theft
There are lots of times when having your tools easily identified is useful. If you are etching or marking for theft reduction, consider using a name or initials instead of or in addition to art. Letters work better in the police reports and on a radio, and are searchable. A nice little etch might make someone pass it by; pawn shops and online buyers will ask a lot more questions, and a thief won't really want to get caught with someone else's stuff. A lot of burglars are caught with goods from several jobs, and if your tools are in the mix, you might get lucky and get them back. If you tried removing an etch or mark, you know it can be s a lot of work to remove it, and bring it back to the factory finish.

Borrowing & Loans
For work or shop settings where tools can be, um, borrowed, or loaned, a logo, initials, or touch mark is nice. A little reminder.

Impact Stencils
If you just need to add a small etch to groups of tools, impact stencils might be the way to go. They are hand written so not as crisp as a computer, but very easy and fast. Tools can be marked for each work station, or job site.

Odd Shapes
If you are doing small or odd shaped tools, lay it on your base plate, and use a gloved hand to hold the stencil while you mark or light etch it, or tape it down to the base plate. The Elmer's Re-Stick applied to the whole stencil does a good job holding the stencil too. For deeper etching, tape or glue down both ends. For curved surfaces, hold the stencil over the curve and dab the stencil over each part to make sure it's all covered.

Surface Texture
A lot of tools are cast, and have a texture. It can be hard to etch or mark on a rough patch, and detail is lost in the bumps, but larger letters are better.

Plated Tools
Many tools are plated with chrome or nickel or something else. Usually they can be marked with saltwater and vinegar. If you etch, you might find it will cut through the plating and expose other metals under it. For marking on plated metal, lower power works better than higher power.

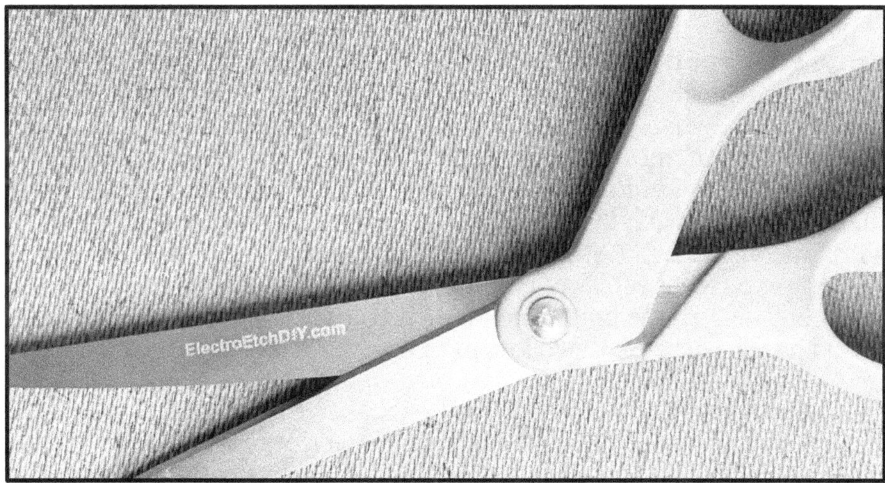

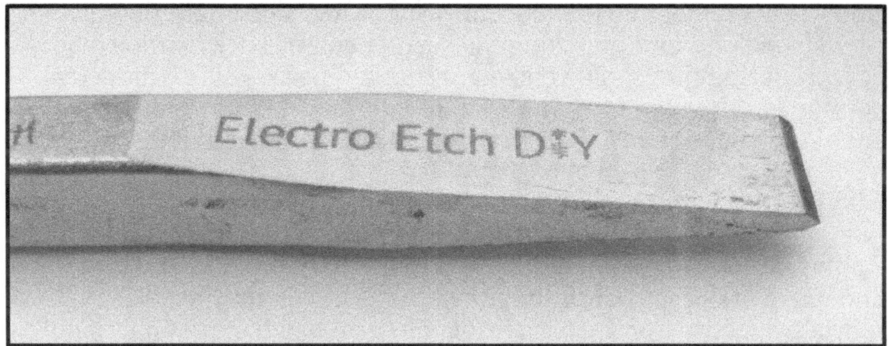

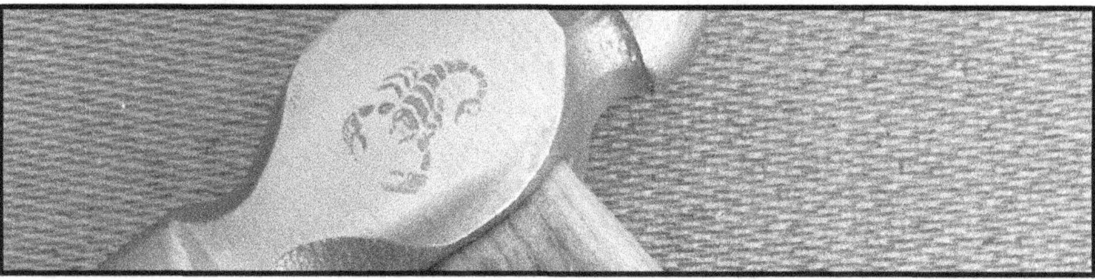

Electro Etch a Knife

Etching or marking a knife is easy, and knife makers and factories have been doing it a long time; lots of the information on electro etching is by knife makers.

Etch Depth, Mark, and Wear
An etch or mark is durable. Most knives do not get a lot of wear except along the cutting edge, and a little up from that, and a mark will not scrub out with daily cleaning. Carbon steel knives will patina and the mark will not have the contrast like on stainless. Some blades are sharpened on the flat with a big stone and will need a deeper etch, or maybe won't handle an etch.

Vinyl vs Screen vs Thermal
A vinyl stencil will allow for the deepest etch but has limited detail. A screen is best when you are doing lots of the same art and also allows a deeper etch than thermal. Thermal stencils are great for normal etching and any kind of mark. Thermal stencils will create an etch that will pretty much last as long as the knife does. Attach the stencil with tape or Elmer's Re-Stick and make sure the stencil is laying flat, and any exposed steel is covered by the stencil or tape. Make sure not to get any electrolyte under the blade if you are using the base plate. With an alligator clip, that's less of a problem.

Existing Finish
A mark will work on high polish steel since it does not make a haze or halo. If you are decorating factory knives, a mark is better than an etch since a regular etch almost always creates a fine halo that has to be polished out, and matching the surface can be tricky. Some blades have a coating that can be etched or marked because it's conductive, but it may or may not turn out. There are lots and lots of coatings, and if the etch or mark doesn't work with it, it's hard to fix.

Electrolyte
Use saltwater with vinegar, or saltwater with baking soda for deep etching. One of these should make a good mark or etch. You might find one works a lot better than the other, or, you may need a specialty electrolyte. Knives use lots of small batch steels that might need something special for good electro etching. The place you bought the steel can maybe tell you the best electrolyte, or, call one of the etch supply outfits and ask.

Setup
Put your blade on a couple of blocks to raise it up if you need to attach an alligator clip. A plastic jig or wood blocks maybe.

Remove the Salts

Wipe down the etch or mark with ammonia solution then with a wet paper towel to get the salts out. If you are using a steel that rusts, make sure to oil it. Ammonia solution helps neutralize the salts for rust prone steels. For important work, scrub with a wet toothbrush.

Haze, Halo & Fuzz

After etching, it may have a haze or oxides. Use Mother's polish on it with a swab; it will clean it right up, or a fine grit Sandflex block, or fine sandpaper. It will take some experience to match the finish.

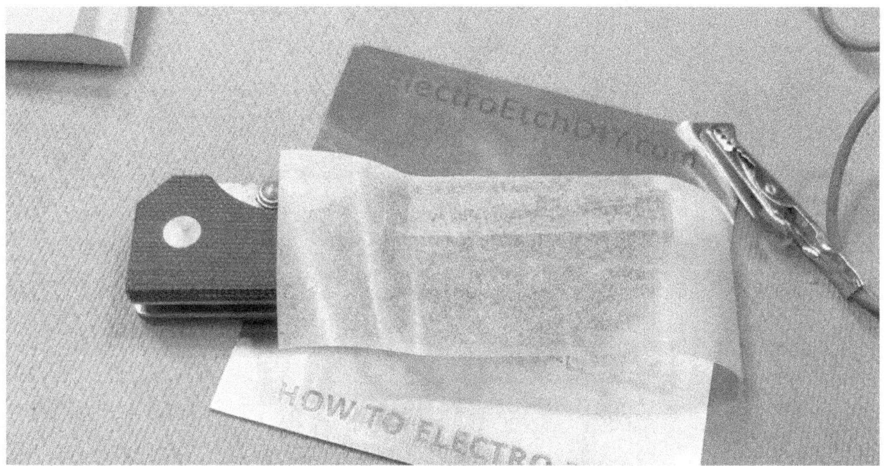

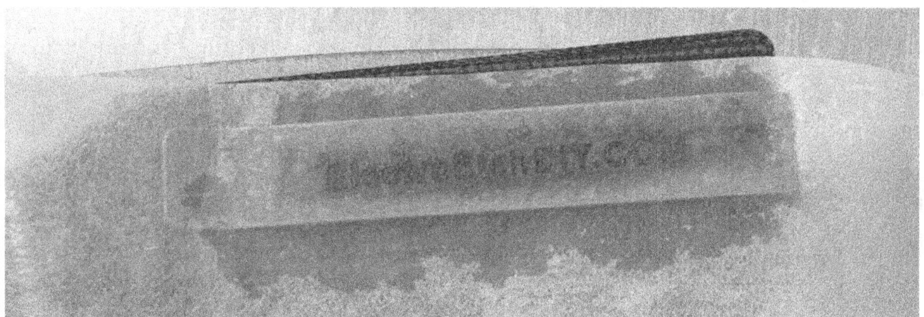

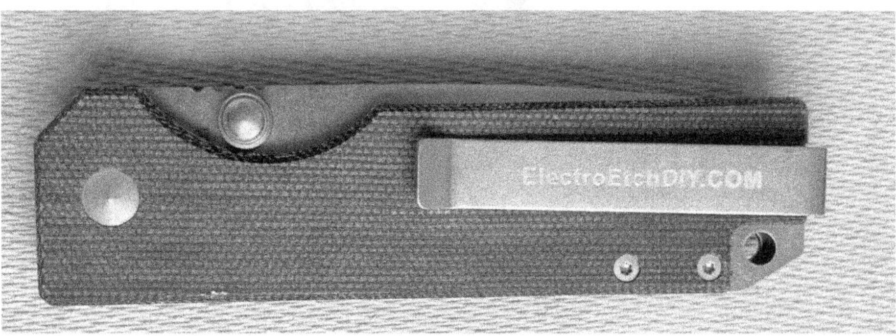

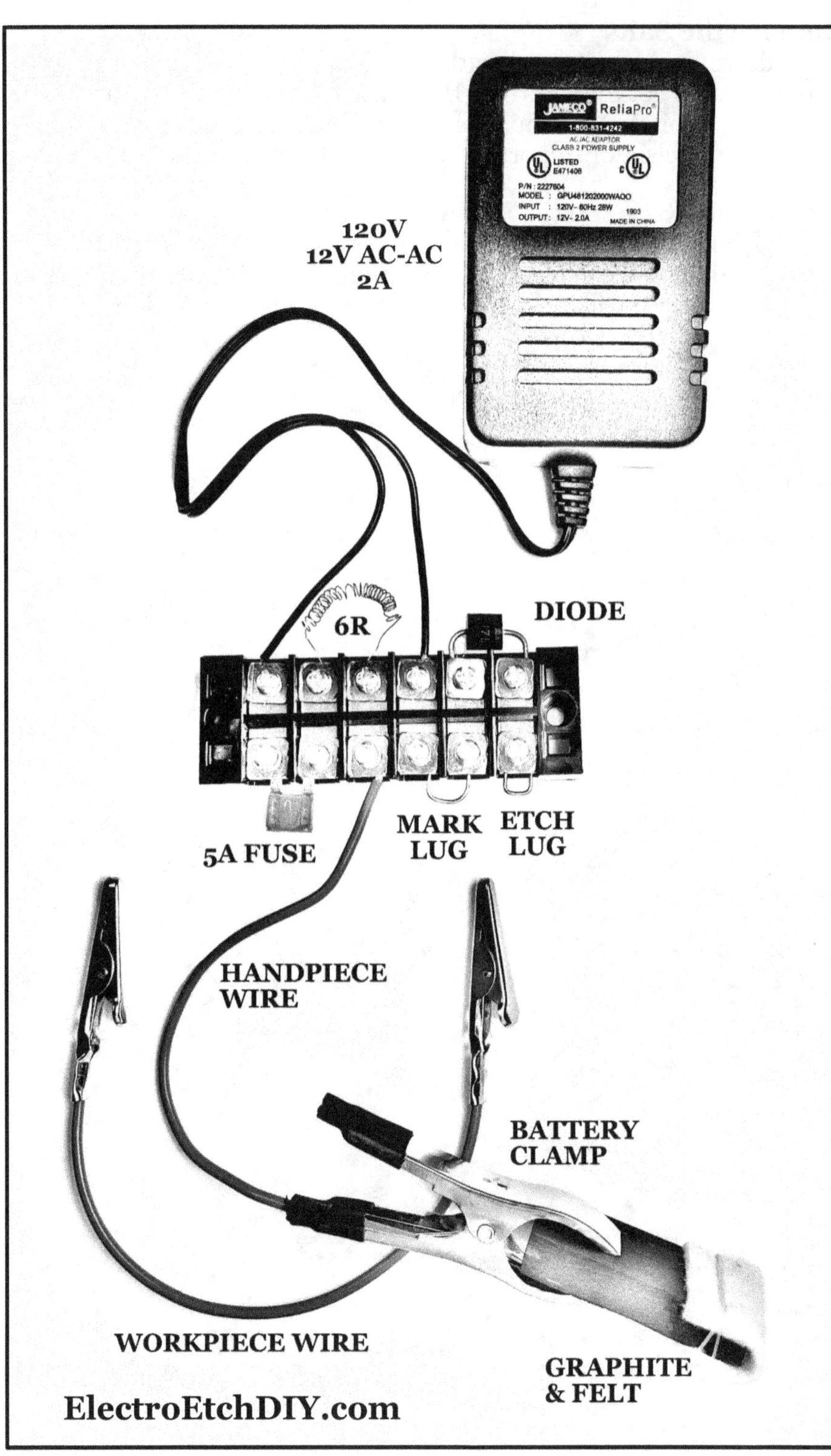

120V
12V AC-AC
2A
Jameco ReliaPro
1-800-831-4242
AC-AC ADAPTOR
CLASS 2 POWER SUPPLY
LISTED
E471408
P/N : 2227804
MODEL : GPU481202000WAOO
INPUT : 120V~ 60Hz 28W
OUTPUT: 12V~ 2.0A
MADE IN CHINA
6R
DIODE
5A FUSE
MARK LUG
ETCH LUG
HANDPIECE WIRE
BATTERY CLAMP
WORKPIECE WIRE
GRAPHITE & FELT
ElectroEtchDIY.com

INDEX

C

D

E

F

G

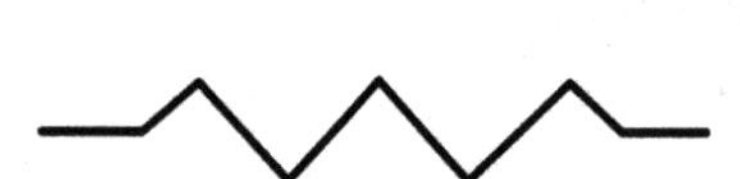